Managing Stress
Stress
WITH Qigong

of related interest

Chinese Medical Qigong
Editor in Chief: Tianjun Liu, O.M.D.
Associate Editor in Chief: Kevin W. Chen, Ph.D.
ISBN 978 1 84819 023 8

Managing Depression with Qigong
Frances Gaik
ISBN 978 1 84819 018 4

Qigong for Multiple Sclerosis
Finding Your Feet Again
Nigel Mills
ISBN 978 1 84819 019 1

Traditional Chinese Medicine Approaches to Cancer
Harmony in the Face of the Tiger
Henry McGrath
ISBN 978 1 84819 013 9

Seeking the Spirit of The Book of Change
8 Days to Mastering a Shamanic Yijing (I Ching) Prediction System
Master Zhongxian Wu
ISBN 978 1 84819 020 7

GORDON FAULKNER

Managing
Stress
WITH Qigong

*Forewords by Carole Bridge
and Patrick Zentler-Munro*

SINGING
DRAGON

LONDON AND PHILADELPHIA

First published in 2011
by Singing Dragon
an imprint of Jessica Kingsley Publishers
116 Pentonville Road
London N1 9JB, UK
and
400 Market Street, Suite 400
Philadelphia, PA 19106, USA

www.singing-dragon.com

Copyright © Gordon Faulkner 2011
Photographs © Niall Hepburn 2011
Forewords © Carole Bridge and Patrick Zentler-Munro 2011

Library of Congress Cataloging in Publication Data
A CIP catalog record for this book is available from the Library of Congress

British Library Cataloguing in Publication Data
A CIP catalogue record for this book is available from the British Library

ISBN 978 1 84819 035 1

Printed and bound in Great Britain by
MPG Books Group

This book is dedicated to Professor Zhang Guangde (张广德).
A modern day master of an ancient tradition.

Acknowledgements

A great many people helped me with this book either knowingly or unknowingly and my thanks go out all of them. Two in particular I will name, my daughter Tina who posed for the photographs to provide a welcome relief from pictures of me. And Niall Hepburn whose camera work graces the pages here.

Here I also acknowledge that any mistakes that appear in this book are mine and not my teachers'.

Contents

Foreword by Carole Bridge   9

Foreword by Patrick Zentler-Munro   11

PREFACE   13

Introduction   15
  Specific or non-specific?   15
  Stress   18
  Background to Daoyin   23

Practice   27
  Basic movements   27
  Standing Stress Relief routine   36
  Seated Stress Relief routine   88
  Standing Stress Prevention routine 128
  Seated Stress Prevention routine 154

Principles of Action 185

    General Principles of Action 185

    Specific Principles of Action 192

    Stress Relief Principles of Action 195

    Stress Prevention Principles of Action 208

APPENDIX A: FIVE ELEMENTS (WUXING) 221

APPENDIX B: ENERGY SYSTEM 227

APPENDIX C: CHINESE NAMES 245

GLOSSARY 249

INDEX 253

List of Diagrams and Tables

Diagrams

1. Three Stages Flow Chart 20

2. Five Stages of Stress 22

3. Five Element Generating Cycle 223

4. Five Element Cruciform Arrangement 224

5. Five Element Controlling Cycle 224

6. Five Element Correspondences 225

Table

1. Five Element Correspondences 221

Foreword

QIGONG AT MAGGIE'S

Maggie's Cancer Caring Centres exist to help people find answers to questions such as: "How am I going to deal with this?"; "What should I ask the doctor?"; "Who can I turn to?"; "Is there anything I can do to help with my treatment and to feel better?"

We provide information and support to address every aspect of living with cancer – from the practicalities of claiming benefits, to the physical and emotional effects that may be experienced. Our aim is to help people manage the impact of cancer and to help people live with hope and determination.

Maggie's is a charity and all of our services are free, which include Qigong as an integral part of the support programme offered at all of our Centres throughout Scotland, and in our newer Centres in England and Wales. Gordon has been working with people affected by cancer at Maggie's Highlands for the past three years.

Most sessions last around an hour and are available for anyone who has cancer or is caring for someone with cancer. The sessions enable people affected by cancer to work with an experienced practitioner and learn simple "meditative" exercises to aid relaxation and to help keep the mind calm and focused. Everyone, whatever their age or physical ability, is able to find exercises which help relaxation. To relax is to conserve energy – Qigong allows people affected by cancer to learn to use a well-balanced interplay of tension and release that is usually associated with general well-being and emotional stability.

Each session is tailored to meet the needs of those attending, according to their experience of Qigong and the level of exercise each person is able to do. This is an essential approach to supporting people affected by cancer, as everyone finds their own way of getting what they need from the programme offered at Maggie's.

I am sure Gordon's book will provide a greater insight for all into the benefits of Qigong for stress, but our experience of the support he offers as part of our programme at Maggie's Highlands is that of positive results for people affected by cancer. There have been many who have participated at some stage of their experience of cancer, and who continue to practise the techniques they have learned from Gordon, as part of their adjustment to either living with their cancer and beyond cancer, or continuing to support a loved one.

Carole Bridge
Centre Head, Maggie's Highlands
www.maggiescentres.org

Foreword

I am an ordinary physician – as critical as most of my colleagues of "complementary therapy." About two years ago I had very extensive surgery for cancer and was left depressed, debilitated, but – so far – free of cancer. Somehow, I found myself attending the local Maggie's Centre – a place which I would previously not have considered setting foot in, even had I developed cancer. And then, I found myself attending Gordon's Qigong class – again, not an activity I could have imagined taking part in even in my wildest dreams!

And, two years later, I am still going… Why? Most obviously because, from the start – weak as I was – the movements made me *feel* better. Perhaps, as the physician in me argued, it was just the passage of time. But as I listened to Gordon, who has studied so much at the feet of the "great masters" in China, I began to understand both the history and the rationale behind each movement. Things began to make sense not only in terms of the constructs of Chinese medicine and philosophy, but also in terms of the science of Western medicine – as Gordon so beautifully explains in his book. I suspect that most of us need things to "make sense," rather than only to be time-honoured, and this is where Gordon's book makes a unique contribution.

Many Chinese hospitals have a Qigong department that offers therapy as part of what we would call "physiotherapy" after most illnesses or operations. I think we probably should do so in our hospitals – and continue at home, as I am – as a means of keeping our organs healthy, as well as exercising our muscles (so much more fun than the gym!) and, perhaps, developing parts of ourselves that "other activities don't reach" – parts we may not know we have.

No double-blind placebo controlled trials to satisfy the authorities – but beautiful, absorbing and quite possibly life-enhancing. Why not read Gordon's guide and give it a try?

Patrick Zentler-Munro MA MD (Cantab) FRCP (Edin)

Preface

Over the last few years I have received many calls to write a book about Daoyin Stress Reduction methods, especially from people who have benefited from the practice and who either wanted detailed information for themselves or wanted to see the benefits passed on to others. Positive feedback arrives constantly about the effectiveness of these exercises but the feedback that is particularly encouraging comes from the Maggie's Cancer Caring Centres that have adopted these exercises as part of their support programme for people struggling with major health issues.

However, the road to this book actually begins much earlier, in May 2005 at the International Daoyin Qigong Symposium in Portugal.

During a meeting with the presidents of the European Daoyin Yangsheng Federation, Madame Zhou Jin, the representative for the Beijing Sports University, made the observation that there were now more teachers in Europe than in Beijing and that we Europeans should stop looking constantly to Beijing for our training and teachers. She looked directly at me and said "You should not rely on the university to teach you the fourth Taiji palm." I was taken by surprise and answered, "I did not know there was a *fourth* Taiji palm," to which she responded, "There isn't until *you* create it." She then went on to remind us that some of us at the table had been officially recognised and designated as the next generation of teachers whose function was not just to spread the knowledge but to *add* to it, specifically to create Daoyin routines for our individual countries' healthcare needs.

Until that point I had been quite happy to be a follower of the ancient and modern traditions of Daoyin. But, as they say, the seed had been planted. The water came from a different source.

That source was an invitation to be a presenter at the 37th International Traditional Chinese Medicine Kongress at Rothenburg ob der Tauber in Germany the following year. The theme of the 37th Kongress was to be "Stress."

Curiously, as I am one of those people who work better under stress/pressure, I set myself a deadline to create a Daoyin stress management system that I could unveil at that Kongress.

It took me a full year of research to work out the Chinese medical theory of what was needed, but then only a few weeks to develop the exercises to fit that theory. It only took a short time to develop the exercises because there is an enormous "back catalogue" of Daoyin routines in existence. I only needed to select the required type and then make slight adjustments to make exercises conform to the theory. As someone told me once, "Don't waste time reinventing the wheel."

So, I present here an old wheel with new treads.

Introduction

Specific or non-specific?

There is a problem with the title of this book, *Managing Stress with Qigong*, because "Managing Stress" seems quite specific enough but "Qigong" is certainly non-specific.

Qigong is an umbrella term for any exercise of the Qi or breath. However, saying I practise Qigong is like saying I play a ball game – what ball game? Tennis? Soccer? Pool? Golf? Each of those ball games, and dozens of others, has its own rules and regulations that distinguish it from the rest. Each type of Qigong has its own rules and regulations too.

In China if anyone says they practise Qigong they also qualify the statement with the name of the style or type of Qigong that they are doing. With this in mind, what we are presenting here is the type of Qigong called Daoyin, which is the oldest and largest subdivision of Qigong, and we make it even more specific when we give it its full title of Daoyin Yangsheng – more will be said of this later.

There is a problem with the expression "physical fitness" because at first glance it seems specific enough but when trying to define what physical fitness means, depending on what authority you consult, you get many different answers. True enough, the core meaning is the same but as the physical fitness industry grows there is a whole host of additions to this core.

In order to become physically fit we have to exercise, but there is a fundamental difference between the goals of physical exercise in the West and the goals of physical exercise in the Orient.

Physical exercise in the West has primarily been concerned with competition – bigger, better, faster, stronger, etc. – a legacy of the Olympic Games, while the Oriental aims have been towards getting healthy. However, there is now movement in the Orient towards exercise for competition and in the West towards exercise for health.

There is a problem with the definition for health. In 1948 the World Health Organization specifically defined health as "a state of complete physical, mental and social well-being and not merely the absence of disease or infirmity." There is definitely a Yin within the Yang here – a specific statement about something non-specific (well-being). This definition seems to be designed to make the job of a physician (the person we entrust with our health) almost impossible. Unless the physician is actually living our life for us he cannot possibly know what *well-being* means to us.

In the West physical fitness has become the order of the day, but being physically fit is not the same as being healthy. Every day there are *very fit* people who get sick and some of them even die. This is in marked contrast to those *very healthy* people who tend not to get sick.

Health clubs abound. Full of state-of-the-art equipment which primarily works the cardiovascular system, I have yet to see any machine in any health club whose purpose is to make the Gallbladder function better; no machine for the Pancreas; no machine for the Spleen; no machine for the Small or Large Intestine; no machine for the Liver or Kidneys, etc.

It should be clear to most people that health is not just about cardiovascular activity. However, given the non-specific nature of everything it is not surprising that there is confusion and conflicting ideas about health, fitness and stress.

Dealing with stress has become very big business with hundreds of stress management companies and specialists offering various methods to combat this problem, and despite their best efforts the annual statistics show increasing numbers of people suffering from stress every year. Stress specialists stand like King Canute against the rising tide of stress and cannot stop it. Why is this?

Because, there is a problem with stress as it is a *non-specific illness.*

A stressor, the cause of stress, can make some people ill and yet at the same time can have a positive effect on others. To use a simple analogy: if the sun is considered to be the stressor, then getting a suntan can be seen as a positive result while getting sunburned is a negative result – stressed.

This positive or negative reaction to the stressor makes it very difficult to pin down "stress" when we are looking for some kind of universal coping method. We have seen that a stressor can have a good or bad action on an individual therefore we need to turn our attention away from the stressor and on to the *reaction* to the stressor.

Ideally, people suffering from stress need to identify the stressor and set about removing it. However, even when the stressor has been correctly identified it is not always possible to remove it – for example, work, caring for elderly parents, or, as in our analogy, the sun, so the next best thing is to come up with an adaptive or coping mechanism to deal with our reaction to the stressor. Continuing with our analogy, removing the sun is not an option, therefore a method to deal with this reaction would be to put ointment on the sunburn as a "stress relief" mechanism and use sun-block as a "stress prevention" mechanism.

The system presented in this book is a physical one aimed at physically active people, although many of the practitioners of this system at the cancer care centres who are undergoing radiation or chemotherapy would dispute the *physically active* label.

It is common knowledge that Chinese exercises such as Taijiquan and Qigong are very good for dealing with stress. However, this is like saying that soccer is very good for fitness – yes it is – but that is not its purpose, that is serendipity.

The Qigong in this book was designed with a very specific purpose in mind and that purpose was to deal with the non-specific condition called chronic stress.

Stress

Stress can be categorized as either acute or chronic. An activity such as dashing across a busy road can arouse an acute, short-term stress reaction but it generally has no long-term effects. However, when the stress is intense, continuous and long lasting, that is, chronic, it has a detrimental effect on an individual.

We are not going to deal with individual cases, symptoms or types of stress. Instead, we will examine the general nature of chronic stress and we will look at it first from a Western viewpoint and then from the Oriental viewpoint.

As has been noted, stress is non-specific. Look at just some of its symptoms: anger, anxiety, breathlessness, chest pains, constipation or diarrhoea, depression, dizziness, loss of appetite, loss of libido, muscle spasms, sleeplessness, tiredness, lack of concentration. There is no constant condition or set of circumstances that can be identified as stress. Having said that, every individual who is suffering from chronic stress usually knows what their particular stressor is.

Hans Selye, the scientist whose groundbreaking work led to our understanding of stress, also noted the great number of confusing definitions which have been conjured up for the word stress. He defined stress as "the non-specific response of the body to any demand." That demand made upon the body, whether it is playing poker, fighting off an infection, or confronting a wild animal, produces a non-specific response which can lead to positive or negative outcomes.

Whether or not the stress is caused by pleasant or unpleasant things, and whether or not it results in good or bad things, stress is the automatic response of the body to make changes in order to adapt to any demand. What can be a problem is not the nature of the demand but our response to it.

The General Adaptive Syndrome (G.A.S.), now more commonly known as the stress syndrome, is the mechanism by which the body confronts stress and is considered to have three stages.

- Stage 1 is the "alarm" or onset phase when the body prepares itself for "fight or flight." This is an acute aroused state.

- Stage 2 is the "resistance" phase where the body has to adapt to ensure that the aroused condition is maintained for longer periods than in the acute state.

- Stage 3 is the "exhaustion" phase where the stress is becoming chronic and the body can no longer cope.

An example of these three stages would be: 1) warming up prior to playing a game; 2) playing the game; and 3) becoming tired during playing the game.

It is because the same stressor can produce different responses in different people that there is a plethora of Stress Reduction techniques with varying degrees of success. So, how does one go about increasing the chance of success? It is the belief offered here that the Oriental approach to dealing with stress gives us greater prospects for recovery.

Looking at the three-stage model from an Oriental point of view requires us to take a Yin and Yang approach. In this instance, Yin refers to the mental response and Yang refers to the physical response.

The stage 1 alarm phase is Yin and the stage 2 resistance phase is Yang. In everyday life, individuals go through the first two stages time and again and this is normal and even desirable (a Taiji balance); what is not desirable, of course, is the severe or chronic stress that leads to the exhaustion in stage 3.

When stage 3 is reached we have the option of collapsing or coping. The positive approach is to find a coping mechanism and with the Oriental system this mechanism has two interdependent parts, Yin and Yang.

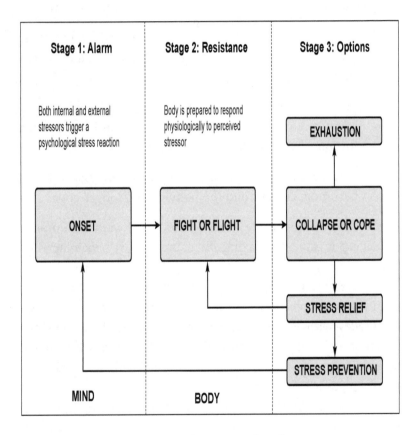

Diagram 1: Three Stages Flow Chart

From the diagram it can be seen that the Stress Relief exercises are designed to deal with stage 2 situations. Because the body systems are moved into "overdrive" at stage 2, the Stress Relief exercises are Yang in nature and involve a certain amount of physical exertion in order to respond positively to the fight or flight expectations of the body.

The Stress Prevention exercises, on the other hand, are designed to be used during stage 1 conditions. Adhering to the old Chinese belief that prevention is better than cure, the Stress Prevention exercises are Yin in nature and are designed to calm the mind down at stress onset and alter our perception of that stress to give a positive result.

Another way of looking at the Stress Reduction process can be seen in Diagram 2, which expands the three-stage view into a five-stage view.

The first part shows the equilibrium of a stress-free situation where the mind and body are united and provide a home for the spirit.

Part 2 shows the arrival of stress acting on the mind creating disharmony which forces a separation from the body leaving no home for the spirit to rest in.

The third part illustrates the action of the Stress Relief exercises which begin to move the body back towards the mind but the Stress Relief itself cannot stop the stress from acting on the mind.

Part 4 shows how the Stress Prevention exercises can create a barrier to the perceived stress but they do little to bring the mind and body together again.

The fifth part illustrates equilibrium in a stressful situation where once again the mind and body are united and provide a home for the spirit with the Stress Relief and Stress Prevention exercises helping to maintain this state.

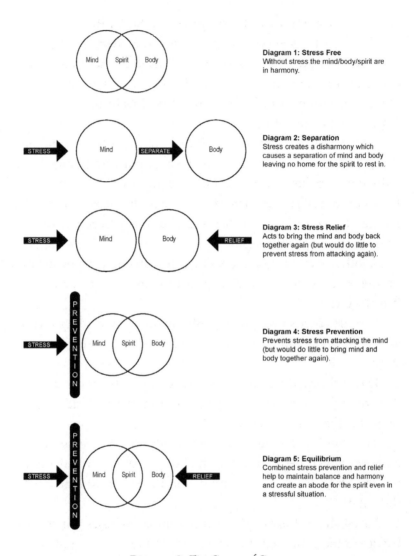

Diagram 1: Stress Free
Without stress the mind/body/spirit are in harmony.

Diagram 2: Separation
Stress creates a disharmony which causes a separation of mind and body leaving no home for the spirit to rest in.

Diagram 3: Stress Relief
Acts to bring the mind and body back together again (but would do little to prevent stress from attacking again).

Diagram 4: Stress Prevention
Prevents stress from attacking the mind (but would do little to bring mind and body together again).

Diagram 5: Equilibrium
Combined stress prevention and relief help to maintain balance and harmony and create an abode for the spirit even in a stressful situation.

Diagram 2: Five Stages of Stress

Both the Stress Relief and the Stress Prevention exercises take approximately ten minutes and are composed of eight gentle movements involving breath control, the stimulation of key acupoints in the body, self-massage and mental focus. The exercises were created using traditional therapeutic movements guided by the theories of Traditional Chinese Medicine, such as

Yin and Yang and the Five Elements, and energy (Qi) circulation through the body's channels or meridians, as they pertain to stress. Please see Appendix B for further information about the meridian system.

Background to Daoyin

Currently the name Qigong is employed as an umbrella term for many different types of exercise with many different purposes. The type of Qigong in this book is Daoyin Yangsheng and it uses physical exercise therapeutically. Physical therapy in the West is concerned mainly with physical problems while in the Orient physical therapy goes beyond this to encompass all types of illness in both preventative and curative modes.

Daoyin is classified as part of both traditional medical knowledge and the practices pertaining to Yangsheng, nourishing the vital principle or nourishing life. Yangsheng itself was also integrated into Daoist practice. Throughout history there have been many types of Qigong, the name and emphasis varying according to the individual purpose. However, its oldest and most diverse type is Daoyin. Dao, to guide, refers to the fact that physical movements are guided by the focus of the mind which, in turn, stimulates the internal flow of Qi within the body. Yin, to pull, means that with the aid of physical movements, Qi can be pulled throughout the body to the appropriate area.

Just a brief look at the highlights of the continuous Daoyin development over the last few thousand years shows the significance of these exercises in Oriental culture. Fads come and go but people would not pursue these exercises uninterruptedly for several millennia if there were no therapeutic benefits.

Most of the texts that mention Daoyin are collected in the Daozang, the Daoist canon, which was only edited in the Ming Dynasty (1368–1644). However, much earlier, on some copperware from the Shang Dynasty (1766–1122 BC) and the Western Zhou Dynasty (1122–771 BC), there are pictures which show people practising Qigong. During the Spring and Autumn Period (770–476 BC) and the Warring States Period (475–221 BC), the "hundred schools of thought" era, Daoyin developed into a fairly systematic art which recommended regulating breathing and the combining of medical treatments with physical exercise.

By the Han Dynasty (206 BC–220 AD) the therapeutic aspects of Daoyin exercises were well established and it received widespread recognition and many of its texts were written in this period. Even the oldest existing document on the subject, the *Daoyin tu* (*Daoyin Exercises Illustrated*) from 168 BC, presents Daoyin's therapeutic aspect. Xi Kang (223–262), author of *Yangsheng lun* (*On Nourishing Life*), introduces the idea that the concentrated mind is a prerequisite for effective results.

The greatest addition to Daoyin theory occurred in the year 610 with the publication of *Zhubing yuanhou lun* (*Treatise on the Causes and Symptoms of Diseases*) which lists hundreds of Daoyin exercises and classifies them in accordance with the origins and symptoms of given medical conditions. These new classifications meant that any Yangsheng or Daoyin practitioner now had a manual in which to look up any exercise and its given indications.

Daoyin was elevated to become an official part of the court medicine in the Tang Dynasty (618–907). Another new development occurred in the Tang Dynasty when Sima Chengzhen (655–735) wrote the *Xiuzhen jingyi zalun* (*Miscellaneous Discourses on the Essential Meaning of Cultivating Perfection*) which introduced the requirement for exercises to be performed *in the correct sequence* if they were to be effective in curing disease and maintaining health.

The only work in the Daoist Canon that deals exclusively with Daoyin is the 4th century *Taiqing daoyin yangsheng jing* (*Great Clarity Scripture of Daoyin and Nourishing Life*). This text is of great significance for the student of the Daoyin tradition in China.

The period between the Tang and Ming Dynasties saw continuous Daoyin activity but with no important developments. But, during the Ming and Qing Dynasties (1644–1911) there was a surge of interest in Qigong in medical circles and many physicians became involved in it. Towards the end of the Qing Dynasty Qigong slipped into decline until in the 1950s it resurfaced and slowly became popular again, but this time not only in China but all over the world.

In the 1970s Daoyin Yangsheng enters the picture. Daoyin Yangsheng is a modern healthcare system created by Professor Zhang Guangde and taught at the Beijing Sports University. This comprehensive system follows the usual Daoyin actions of gentle exercise with breath control, the stimulation of key acupoints in the body, self massage and mental development but has now been updated by combining Traditional Chinese Medicine with modern knowledge of anatomy, physiology and medical theory.

Professor Zhang made a keen study of the classical theories of the Daoyin, Yangsheng and Longevity schools. He had inherited a family owned "Exercises for Chronic Diseases" from his maternal grandfather and started the development of modern Daoyin Yangsheng when he, himself, was severely ill. Basing his work on this huge wealth of traditional knowledge, Professor Zhang developed his new style to combine the methods of Daoyin with physical exercise and mental cultivation. It was through the use of this health system, so it is claimed, that the Professor overcame his own illnesses.

These exercises are guided by the theories of Traditional Chinese Medicine such as the concept of holism, the theory of diagnosis and treatment based on differential analysis of symptoms and signs, the ancient theories of Yin and Yang (energetic polarities) and the Five Elements (see Appendix A) and Qi circulation through the energy system (see Appendix B), and the aetiology and pathology of diseases and related studies of modern medicine.[1]

Today, Daoyin Yangsheng is part of the Chinese National Fitness Programme. The Chinese Olympic Committee recommends it for its athletes and the Chinese Wushu Association considers it to be a premier healthcare system.

---

1   For a detailed history of Daoyin see Kohn, Livia (2008) *Chinese Healing Exercises*. Honolulu: University of Hawaii Press.

Practice

The Daoyin Yangsheng branch of the Chanquanshu School of Daoist Arts teaches Daoyin to three levels and, although there is a great deal of information in this book, we only explore level 1. More information on Daoyin Yangsheng training can be found at www.daoyin.co.uk.

Basic movements

Before starting the descriptions of the individual exercises we will cover the basic movements and common principles of Daoyin exercises presented in this book.

Hand positions

The most common hand positions in the Daoyin Yangsheng exercises are the palms, the fists and their variations.

CLOSED PALM

Extend the fingers naturally and bring them together with the thumb aligned with them. (Fig. 1)

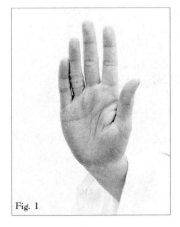

Fig. 1

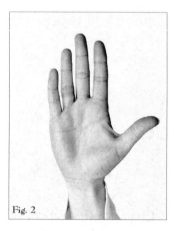

Fig. 2

OPEN PALM

Exactly the same as the closed palm but with the thumb extended away from the fingers. (Fig. 2)

Fig. 3

EIGHT CHARACTER PALM

This is the same as the open palm but with the middle, ring and little fingers bent into the palm. (Fig. 3)

Fig. 4

DRAGON PALM

This palm is similar to the closed palm with the fingers extended naturally and with the thumb aligned with them but now the thumb is below the index finger. (Fig. 4) The webbed area between the thumb and index finger is referred to as the "tigermouth" and takes its name from one of the alternate designations for the acupoint LI-4.

In the Yin palm movements the fingers are kept straight (except for the three in the eight character palm) but relaxed, while in the Yang palm movements the fingers become stretched and slightly pulled back in hyperextension.

HOLLOW FIST

This is similar to a normal fist, but more open, with the four fingers curved inwards with the thumb bent across the fingers, like holding a broom handle. (Fig. 5)

Fig. 5

SHANG FIST

This is similar to the eight character palm with middle, ring and little fingers bent, but now the index finger and thumb are bent to touch each other so that the Shaoshang LU-11 acupoint of the thumb connects with the Shangyang LI-1 acupoint of the index finger. (Fig. 6, 7)

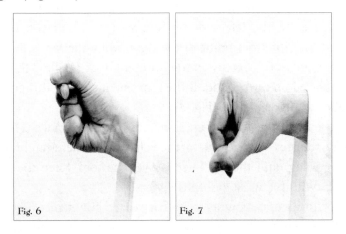

Fig. 6

Fig. 7

BALL HOLDING

The ball holding posture used here is where the hands are placed one above the other as though holding something the size of a beach ball to the front of the chest. (Fig. 11 shows ball holding in horse stance)

Daoyin Stepping

Every step results in a stance and, while the stances used in Daoyin are generally the same as in Wushu, Chinese martial arts, the method of stepping into them is specific to Daoyin; that is, stepping forward looks the same in Taijiquan as it does in Daoyin but it is performed slightly differently. The descriptions that follow start in the feet together posture and have the stepping action performed by the left leg.

DIAGONAL STEPPING

Diagonal Stepping is used to move into the toe-up stance, the bow stance and the twisted bow stance.

Move the centre of gravity to the right foot, bend the right leg slightly and raise the left heel. Without pause, turn the body 45 degrees to the left and step out to the left diagonal with the left foot; the toes point to the floor while the leg is moving forward and at full extension the toes pull back to allow the heel to be placed on the ground. If the movement stops at this point it is called a toe-up stance. (Fig. 8)

To move from the toe-up stance into a bow stance (Fig. 9), slowly transfer the weight to the left foot while straightening the right leg until the left knee is over the toes. Keep the torso upright with the waist and hips lowered.

To move from a bow stance into a twisted bow stance (Fig. 10), keep the feet and legs still but turn the torso fully to the left side.

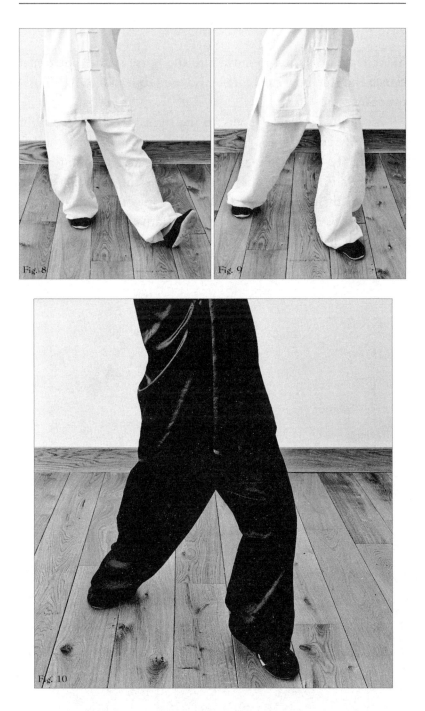

Fig. 8

Fig. 9

Fig. 10

SIDE STEPPING

Side Stepping is used to move into the horse stance, horizontal stance and side bow stance. It is also used to lead into the Crossover Stepping.

Move the centre of gravity to the right foot, bend the right leg slightly and raise the left heel. Without pause, move the left foot directly to the side, with the big toe still pointing at the ground, and then place the foot down, toes first, parallel to the right foot then transfer the bodyweight into the middle. If the distance between the feet is shoulder-width then it is just a side step but if it is wider than this it then becomes a horse stance. (Fig. 11)

Fig. 11

To move from the horse stance into a horizontal stance (Fig. 12), keep the left leg bent and straighten the right leg to transfer the bodyweight onto the left foot.

To move from the horizontal stance into a side bow stance (Fig. 13), keep the left foot still but turn the torso to face the left by pivoting on the ball of the right foot to move the heel to the right.

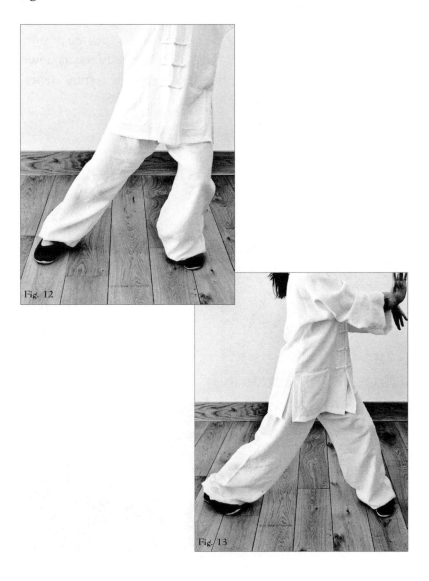

Fig. 12

Fig. 13

CROSS-OVER STEPPING

Cross-over Stepping is used to move into the high and low cross stances and the high and low resting stances.

Move the centre of gravity to the right foot and then move the left foot across to the right either in front or behind and beyond the right foot. Transfer the bodyweight to whichever foot is in front and raise the heel of the rear foot but keep all its toes on the ground.

When the weight is shifted back onto the rear toes the posture becomes a high resting stance. (Fig. 14) If the body squats down to sit on the rear foot the posture is called a low resting stance. (Fig. 15) In both instances the torso is held upright.

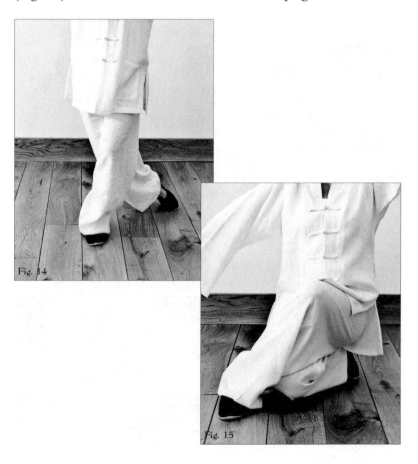

Fig. 14

Fig. 15

Characteristic features of the exercises

1. Combine thought with physical movement, emphasizing thought.

2. Coordinate physical movement with breathing, emphasizing breathing.

3. While inhaling, draw up the anus and tilt the pelvis up to the front; while exhaling, relax the anus and relax the abdomen.

4. Inhale and exhale through the nose and keep the tongue on the roof of the mouth throughout.

5. Use a combination of slow and forceful actions.

6. Keep the whole body in continuous motion.

These characteristics are indicative of the coordinated use of mind, body and breath required in Qigong practice.

STANDING STRESS RELIEF ROUTINE

The Stress Relief routine is the Yang half of the Stress Reduction method. Being Yang means that it is more physically demanding than the Yin Stress Prevention routine because it is designed to work with stage 2 of the stress response, the "fight or flight" reaction which prepares the body physiologically for action.

Standing Stress Relief Exercise 1: Taiji Breathing

Starting position: Stand with the feet together, weight evenly distributed, body upright and relaxed with the hands hanging down at the sides of the body. Look straight ahead. (Fig. R.1)

Fig. R.1

Recite silently:

> *In the late evening stillness leave all troubles behind,*
>
> *Set the mind on Dantian and seal the seven openings.*
>
> *Breathe gently and unhurried and raise the magpie bridge,*
>
> *With the body light as a swallow soaring through the skies.*

Part 1

1. INHALING

Raise the anus, tilt the pelvis (see pp.189–190) and draw in the lower abdomen; move the centre of gravity to the right foot, bend the right leg slightly and raise the left heel while rotating the arms outward until both palms face outward from the sides. (Fig. R.2)

Without pause, take a step with the left foot to the left, Daoyin Side Stepping, so that the feet are a little more than shoulder-width apart; move the centre of gravity to a position between both feet (Fig. R.3) and then slowly straighten the legs. Simultaneously, raise the arms sideways until they are over the head with the

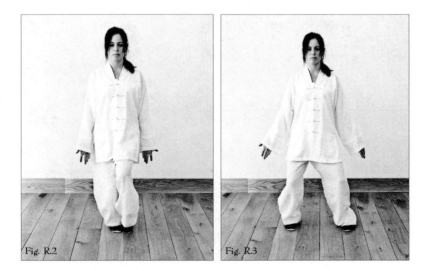

Fig. R.2

Fig. R.3

palms facing acupoint Baihui DU-20 on the crown, fingertips pointing towards each other. Look straight ahead. (Fig. R.4)

2. EXHALING

Relax the anus, relax the pelvis and relax the lower abdomen; bend both legs and slowly squat into a high horse stance. At the same time, lower the arms in front of the body until the hands reach the Lower Dantian with the palms facing downward. Look straight ahead. (Fig. R.5)

Fig. R.4

Fig. R.5

3. INHALING

Raise the anus, tilt the pelvis and draw in the lower abdomen; rotate the arms outward until both palms face out from the sides, then slowly straighten the legs while raising the arms sideways until they are over the head with the palms facing acupoint Baihui DU-20 on the crown, fingertips pointing towards each other. Look straight ahead.

4. EXHALING

Relax the anus, relax the pelvis and relax the lower abdomen; bend both legs and slowly squat into a high horse stance. At the same time, lower the arms in front of the body until the hands reach the Lower Dantian with the palms facing downward. Look straight ahead. This is a repeat of step 2.

5. INHALING

Raise the anus, tilt the pelvis and draw in the lower abdomen; rotate the arms outward until both palms face out from the sides, then slowly straighten the legs while raising the arms sideways until they are over the head with the palms facing acupoint Baihui DU-20 on the crown, fingertips pointing towards each other. Look straight ahead. This is a repeat of step 3.

6. EXHALING

Relax the anus, relax the pelvis and relax the lower abdomen; bend both legs and slowly squat into a high horse stance. At the same time, lower the arms in front of the body until the hands reach the Lower Dantian with the palms facing downward. Look straight ahead. This is a repeat of step 2.

7. INHALING

Raise the anus, tilt the pelvis and draw in the lower abdomen; rotate the arms outward until both palms face out from the sides, then slowly straighten the legs while raising the arms sideways until they are over the head with the palms facing acupoint Baihui DU-20 on the crown, fingertips pointing towards each other. Look straight ahead. This is a repeat of step 3.

8. EXHALING

Relax the anus, relax the pelvis and relax the lower abdomen; move the centre of gravity to the right foot, bend the right leg and straighten the left leg before moving the left foot back to the side of the right foot, and then slowly straighten the legs and bring the centre of gravity to the middle. At the same time, lower the arms in front of the body until the hands reach the Lower Dantian with the palms facing downward, and then bring the hands to the side as in the original starting position. Look straight ahead.

Part 2

Repeat on the right side, reversing all left/right directions.

Main points

1. The purpose of this exercise is to open the sequence; set the breathing, movement and mind in harmony (Three Regulations) for the rest of the routine.

2. The mental focus during this exercise is on the acupoints Laogong PC-8 on the palms of the hands while raising the arms, and then changes to the Lower Dantian in the lower abdomen while lowering the arms.

3.   Throughout the whole exercise, when the arms are being raised the palms become Yang palms and the weight shifts to the balls of the feet, and when the arms are being lowered the palms change to Yin palms and the weight shifts to the heels.

Standing Stress Relief Exercise 2: Swirling Water

Starting position: Stand with the feet together, weight evenly distributed, body upright and relaxed with the hands hanging down at the sides of the body. Look straight ahead. (Fig. R.1)

Part 1

1. INHALING

Raise the anus, tilt the pelvis and draw in the lower abdomen; move the centre of gravity to the right foot, bend the right leg slightly and raise the left heel while sweeping the arms in front of the body until the palms are in front of the hips, palms facing inward. (Fig. R.6)

Fig. R.6

Without pause turn the body 45 degrees to the left, step out with the left foot, Daoyin Diagonal Stepping, to the left diagonal and set the heel on the ground in a toe-up empty stance while raising the hands upwards close to the body to upper chest height, palms still facing inward and fingertips pointing to each other. (Fig. R.7)

Fig. R.7

2. EXHALING

Relax the anus, relax the pelvis and relax the lower abdomen; move the centre of gravity forward to the left foot into a left bow stance and at the same time slowly extend the arms outward in an embracing position. Turn the palms slightly upward and look towards them. (Fig. R.8)

Fig. R.8

3. INHALING

Raise the anus, tilt the pelvis and draw in the lower abdomen; straighten the left leg and transfer the centre of gravity to the bent right leg in a left toe-up empty stance. Simultaneously, turn the body rightward and swing the right arm, palm upward at shoulder height, in an arc to the rear as far as possible. Head and eyes follow the right palm. (Fig. R.9)

Fig. R.9

4. EXHALING

Relax the anus, relax the pelvis and relax the lower abdomen; turn the body leftward, straighten the right leg and transfer the centre of gravity to the left foot into a left bow stance. At the same time, move the right hand to the side of the head, palm forward, fingers

Fig. R.10

pointing left and then push the palm to the front alongside the left palm. Look towards the hands. (Fig. R.10)

5. INHALING

Raise the anus, tilt the pelvis and draw in the lower abdomen; straighten the left leg and transfer the centre of gravity to the bent right leg in a left toe-up empty stance. Simultaneously, turn the body leftward and swing the left arm, palm upward at shoulder height, in an arc to the rear as far as possible. Head and eyes follow the left palm. This is the same as step 3 but with the left arm.

6. EXHALING

Relax the anus, relax the pelvis and relax the lower abdomen; turn the body rightward, straighten the right leg and transfer the centre of gravity to the left foot into a left bow stance. At the same time, move the left hand to the side of the head, palm forward, fingers pointing right and then push the palm to the front alongside the right palm. Look towards the back of the hands. (Fig. R.11) This is the same as step 4 but with the left arm.

Fig. R.11

7. INHALING

Raise the anus, tilt the pelvis and draw in the lower abdomen; straighten the left leg and transfer the centre of gravity to the bent right leg in a left toe-up empty stance. Simultaneously, rotate both palms to face inwards and then turn the body rightward to face the front. (Fig. R.12)

Fig. R.12

8. EXHALING

Relax the anus, relax the pelvis and relax the lower abdomen; bring the left foot to the side of the right, feet together, draw palms close to chest and lower them, returning the body to the starting position.

Part 2

Repeat on right side, reversing all left/right directions.

Main points

1. The purpose of this exercise is to calm the mind.

2. The mental focus during this exercise is on the acupoints Laogong PC-8.

3. When moving the arm to the rear, sweep it as far as possible to feel tightness over the scapula.

Standing Stress Relief Exercise 3: Eagle Soaring in the Sky

Starting position: Stand with the feet together, weight evenly distributed, body upright and relaxed with the hands hanging down at the sides of the body. Look straight ahead. (Fig. R.1)

Part 1

1. INHALING

Raise the anus, tilt the pelvis and draw in the lower abdomen; move the centre of gravity to the right foot, bend the right leg slightly and raise the left heel while both arms rotate outward until the palms face forward. (Fig. R.13)

Fig. R.13

Without pause turn the body 45 degrees to the left, step out with the left foot, Daoyin Diagonal Stepping, to the left diagonal and set the heel on the ground in a left toe-up empty stance. Slowly raise the arms upward to the front to shoulder level, hands moving towards each other until the right palm is over, but not touching, the left palm, palms facing upward. Look towards the hands. (Fig. R.14)

Fig. R.14

2. EXHALING

Relax the anus, relax the pelvis and relax the lower abdomen; toe out the left foot and transfer the centre of gravity to the left leg while lifting the right heel up but keeping all the toes touching the ground and allowing the right leg to twist and stretch straight into a high cross stance. At the same time, rotate the hands so that the fingertips point to the chest (Fig. R.15) and then pass by the armpits to stretch the arms straight, left arm angled down and right arm angled up, with palms facing upward. Look at the rear right foot. (Fig. R.16)

Fig. R.15   Fig. R.16

3. INHALING

Raise the anus, tilt the pelvis and draw in the lower abdomen; twist the right foot back and place the heel back in its starting position. Transfer the centre of gravity onto the right foot and let the left leg return to the toe-up empty stance. Simultaneously, raise the left arm and lower the right arm while swinging them both to the front of the body at shoulder height with palms facing downward. The body now faces forward and the eyes look straight ahead. (Fig. R.17)

Fig. R.17

4. EXHALING

Relax the anus, relax the pelvis and relax the lower abdomen; bring the left foot to the side of the right, feet together, (Fig. R.18) and lower the arms down the front, returning the body to the starting position.

Fig. R.18

5. INHALING

Raise the anus, tilt the pelvis and draw in the lower abdomen; move the centre of gravity to the left foot, bend the left leg slightly and raise the right heel while both arms rotate outward until palms face forward.

Without pause turn the body 45 degrees to the right, step out with the right foot, Daoyin Diagonal Stepping, to the right diagonal and set the heel on the ground in a toe-up empty stance. Slowly raise the arms upward to the front to shoulder level, hands moving towards each other until the left palm is over, but not touching, the right palm, palms facing upward. Look towards the hands. This is a repeat of step 1 performed on the opposite side.

6. EXHALING

Relax the anus, relax the pelvis and relax the lower abdomen; toe out the right foot and transfer the centre of gravity to the right leg while lifting the left heel up but keeping all the toes touching the ground and allowing the left leg to twist and stretch straight into a high cross stance. At the same time, rotate the hands so that the fingertips point to the chest and then pass by the armpits to stretch the arms straight, right arm angled down and left arm angled up, with palms facing upward. Look at the rear left foot. This is a repeat of step 2 performed on the opposite side.

7. INHALING

Raise the anus, tilt the pelvis and draw in the lower abdomen; twist the left foot back and place the heel back in its starting position. Transfer the centre of gravity onto the left foot and let the right leg return to the toe-up empty stance. Simultaneously, raise the right arm and lower the left arm while swinging them both to the front of the body at shoulder height with palms facing downward. The body now faces forward and the eyes look straight ahead. This is a repeat of step 3 performed on the opposite side.

8. EXHALING

Relax the anus, relax the pelvis and relax the lower abdomen; bring the left foot to the side of the right, feet together, and lower the arms down the front, returning the body to the starting position. This is a repeat of step 4 performed on the opposite side.

Part 2

Repeat.

Main points

1. The purpose of this exercise is to eliminate Fire from the Heart and Liver and to dispel Phlegm.

2. The mental focus during this exercise is on the acupoint Mingmen DU-4.

3. When rotating the arms twist them as much as possible.

Standing Stress Relief Exercise 4: Black Dragon Displays Talons

Starting position: Stand with the feet together, weight evenly distributed, body upright and relaxed with the hands hanging down at the sides of the body. Look straight ahead. (Fig. R.1)

Part 1

1. INHALING

Raise the anus, tilt the pelvis and draw in the lower abdomen; move the centre of gravity to the right foot, bend the right leg slightly and raise the left heel while rotating the arms inward until both palms face the rear. (Fig. R.19)

Fig. R.19

Without pause, take a step with the left foot to the left, Daoyin Side Stepping, so that the feet are a little more than shoulder-width apart, transfer the centre of gravity to the bent left leg and straighten the right leg in a left horizontal stance. Simultaneously, raise the arms sideways up to shoulder level and then rotate them until the palms face downward. Look to the left. (Fig. R.20)

Fig. R.20

2. EXHALING

Relax the anus, relax the pelvis and relax the lower abdomen; move the right foot across in front of the left, Daoyin Cross-over Stepping, and transfer the centre of gravity to it in a high cross stance. Simultaneously, swing the arms, at shoulder height, in front of the body with the palms facing downward. Body, arms and head all face the left diagonal. (Fig. R.21)

Fig. R.21

Without pause squat into a low resting stance on the left heel and draw the hands back and down until the right palm is resting on the right thigh at Jimen SP-11 and the left thumb is touching the right foot at Xingjian LR-2 acupoint. The movement concludes with the right side of the chest expanding while the left side contracts and the left thumb presses firmly on acupoint Xingjian LR-2. Look at the right foot. (Fig. R.22)

Fig. R.22

3. INHALING

Raise the anus, tilt the pelvis and draw in the lower abdomen; transfer the centre of gravity onto the right foot, rise up and straighten both legs into a high cross stance. Simultaneously, move both hands upward, close to the chest, to shoulder height and then stretch the fingers wide while pushing the arms forward. Look towards the hands. (Fig. R.23)

Fig. R.23

4. EXHALING

Relax the anus, relax the pelvis and relax the lower abdomen; squat into a low resting stance on the left heel and draw the hands back and down until the right palm is resting on the right thigh at Jimen SP-11 and the left thumb is touching the right foot at Xingjian LR-2 acupoint. The movement concludes with the right side of the chest expanding while the left side contracts and the left thumb presses firmly on acupoint Xingjian LR-2. Look at the right foot.

5. INHALING

Raise the anus, tilt the pelvis and draw in the lower abdomen; transfer the centre of gravity onto the right foot, rise up and straighten both legs into a high cross stance. Simultaneously, move both hands upward, close to the chest, to shoulder height and then stretch the fingers wide while pushing the arms forward. Look towards the hands. This is a repeat of step 3.

6. EXHALING

Relax the anus, relax the pelvis and relax the lower abdomen; squat into a low resting stance on the left heel and draw the hands back and down until the right palm is resting on the right thigh at Jimen SP-11 and the left thumb is touching the right foot at Xingjian LR-2 acupoint. The movement concludes with the right side of the chest expanding while the left side contracts and the left thumb presses firmly on acupoint Xingjian LR-2. Look at the right foot. This is a repeat of step 4.

7. INHALING

Raise the anus, tilt the pelvis and draw in the lower abdomen; transfer the body centre of gravity onto the right foot, rise up and straighten both legs into a high cross stance. Simultaneously, move both hands upward, close to the chest, to shoulder height, palm down with the fingers pointing at each other. (Fig. R.24)

Fig. R.24

Without pause transfer the body centre of gravity onto the left foot, move the right foot back to the right, as in step 1 and then transfer the centre of gravity to it in a right horizontal stance. The arms, meanwhile, spread out to the sides at shoulder height palms down and the head and eyes look towards the right hand. (Fig. R.25)

Fig. R.25

8. EXHALING

Relax the anus, relax the pelvis and relax the lower abdomen; bring the left foot to the side of the right, feet together, and lower the arms down to the sides of the body returning to the starting position. Eyes look directly ahead.

Part 2

Repeat on right side, reversing all left/right directions.

Main points

1. The purpose of this exercise is to eliminate Fire from the Liver and to remove Liver-Qi Stagnation.

2. The mental focus during this exercise is on the acupoints Xingjian LR-2.

3. When spreading the fingers stretch them as far apart as possible.

4. Jimen SP-11 is a point of reference not a point of focus.

Standing Stress Relief Exercise 5: Dragon Hiding in the Blue Sea

Starting position: Stand with the feet together, weight evenly distributed, body upright and relaxed with the hands hanging down at the sides of the body. Look straight ahead. (Fig. R.1)

Part 1

1. INHALING

Raise the anus, tilt the pelvis and draw in the lower abdomen; move the centre of gravity to the right foot, bend the right leg slightly and raise the left heel while rotating the arms outward until both palms face forward. (Fig. R.26)

Without pause, take a step with the left foot to the left, Daoyin Side Stepping, so that the feet are a little more than shoulder-width apart, transfer the centre of gravity to the bent left leg and straighten the right leg in a left horizontal stance. Simultaneously, raise the arms upward to the front to shoulder level, hands moving towards each other until the right palm is resting on the top of the left palm (both palms facing up). Look straight ahead. (Fig. R.27)

2. EXHALING

Relax the anus, relax the pelvis and relax the lower abdomen; keeping the centre of gravity on the left leg, move the right foot across behind the left, Daoyin Cross-over Stepping, resting the ball of the foot on the ground, right leg half squatting in a high resting stance. At the same time, curl the arms in toward the chest and turn the palms over to face downward. (Fig. R.28)

Without pausing, squat into a low resting stance on the right heel and separate the palms. The right palm pushes down and out to the right side while the left arm rotates and pushes upward. Look to the right. (Fig. R.29)

3. INHALING

Raise the anus, tilt the pelvis and draw in the lower abdomen; pushing up from the ground, straighten both legs with the centre of gravity on the left foot. Simultaneously, the arms swing together until the left hand is resting on top of the right hand, palms downward, in front of the chest.

Without pausing, take a step with the right foot back to its starting position; keeping the hands together turn the palms upward while straightening the arms out to the front as the right leg is bent and the left leg stretched straight in a right horizontal stance. Look straight ahead. (Fig. R.30)

Fig. R.26

Fig. R.27

Fig. R.28

Fig. R.29

Fig. R.30

4. EXHALING

Relax the anus, relax the pelvis and relax the lower abdomen; bring the left foot to the side of the right foot and at the same time separate the hands and turn them palm down. (Fig. R.31) Then, without pausing, straighten both legs and lower both arms to return to the starting position. Look straight ahead.

Fig. R.31

5. INHALING

Raise the anus, tilt the pelvis and draw in the lower abdomen; move the centre of gravity to the left foot, bend the left leg slightly and raise the right heel while rotating the arms outward until both palms face forward.

Without pause, take a step with the right foot to the right, Daoyin Side Stepping, so that the feet are a little more than shoulder-width apart, transfer the centre of gravity to the bent right leg and straighten the left leg in a right horizontal stance. Simultaneously, raise the arms upward to the front to shoulder level, hands moving towards each other until the left palm is resting on the top of the right palm. Look straight ahead. This is a repeat of step 1 but in the opposite direction.

6. EXHALING

Relax the anus, relax the pelvis and relax the lower abdomen; keeping the centre of gravity on the right leg, move the left foot across behind the right, Daoyin Cross-over Stepping, resting the ball of the foot on the ground, left leg half squatting in a high resting stance. At the same time, curl the arms in toward the chest and turn the palms over to face downward.

Without pausing, squat into a low resting stance on the left heel and separate the palms. The left palm pushes down and out to the left side while the right arm rotates and pushes upward. Look to the left. This is a repeat of step 2 but in the opposite direction.

7. INHALING

Raise the anus, tilt the pelvis and draw in the lower abdomen; pushing up from the ground, straighten both legs with the centre of gravity on the right foot. Simultaneously, the arms swing together until the right hand is resting on top of the left hand, palms downward, in front of the chest.

Without pausing, move the left foot back to its starting position; keeping the hands together turn the palms upward while straightening the arms out to the front as the left leg is bent and the right leg stretched straight in a left horizontal stance. Look straight ahead. This is a repeat of step 3 but in the opposite direction.

8. EXHALING

Relax the anus, relax the pelvis and relax the lower abdomen; bring the right foot to the side of the left foot and at the same time separate the hands and turn them palm down. Then, without pausing, straighten both legs and lower both arms to return to the starting position. Look straight ahead. This is a repeat of step 4 but in the opposite direction.

Part 2

Repeat.

Main points

1. The purpose of this exercise is to eliminate Fire from the Heart and Liver and to dispel Phlegm.

2. The mental focus during this exercise is on the acupoints Laogong PC-8.

3. When squatting ensure the upper body is vertical. Do not lean forward.

Standing Stress Relief Exercise 6: Swirling Clouds

Starting position: Stand with the feet together, weight evenly distributed, body upright and relaxed with the hands hanging down at the sides of the body. Look straight ahead. (Fig. R.1)

Part 1

1. INHALING

Raise the anus, tilt the pelvis and draw in the lower abdomen; move the centre of gravity to the right foot, bend the right leg slightly and raise the left heel while bending the wrists so that the fingertips are pointing to the hips. (Fig. R.32)

Fig. R.32

Without pause, take a step with the left foot to the left, Daoyin Side Stepping, so that the feet are approximately twice the width of the shoulders apart, move the centre of gravity to a position between both feet and then slowly straighten the legs. Simultaneously, raise the arms sideways until they are at shoulder level with the palms facing down. Then bend the knees and settle into a horse stance. Look straight ahead. (Fig. R.33)

Fig. R.33

2. EXHALING

Relax the anus, relax the pelvis and relax the lower abdomen; slowly transfer the centre of gravity onto the left foot while pivoting on the ball of the right foot to push the heel away as the right leg straightens turning the upper body to face the left in a left side bow stance.

At the same time, swing the right arm upwards then downwards with fingers trailing and the left arm downwards then upwards with fingers trailing until the left Zhigou SJ-6 is firmly pressed against the right Neiguan PC-6, then hyperextend the left hand to point the fingers up and flex the right hand to point the fingers down. Look straight ahead to the left. (Fig. R.34, R.35)

Fig. R.34

Fig. R.35

3. INHALING

Raise the anus, tilt the pelvis and draw in the lower abdomen; pivot on the right foot and bring the heel back to its original position and turn the upper body rightward to face the front with the weight evenly distributed in a horse stance. Simultaneously, lift the right arm, lower the left arm and bring them in front of the chest in the ball holding position. (Fig. R.36)

Without pausing, swing the right arm in an arc upward, outward and downward to the right while the left arm swings in an arc upward and outward to the left until both arms are at shoulder height with palms facing downward. Look to the front.

Fig. R.36

4. EXHALING

Relax the anus, relax the pelvis and relax the lower abdomen; slowly transfer the centre of gravity onto the right foot while pivoting on the ball of the left foot to push the heel away as the left leg straightens turning the upper body to face the right in a right side bow stance.

At the same time, swing the left arm upwards then downwards with fingers trailing and the right arm downwards then upwards with fingers trailing until the right Zhigou SJ-6 is firmly pressed against the left Neiguan PC-6, then hyperextend the right hand to point the fingers up and flex the left hand to point the fingers down. Look straight ahead to the right. This is a repeat of step 2 but on the opposite side, reversing all left/right directions.

5. INHALING

Raise the anus, tilt the pelvis and draw in the lower abdomen; pivot on the left foot and bring the heel back to its original position and turn the upper body leftward to face the front with the weight evenly distributed in a horse stance. Simultaneously, lift the left arm, lower the right arm and bring them in front of the chest in the ball holding position.

Without pausing, swing the left arm in an arc upward, outward and downward to the left while the right arm swings in an arc upward and outward to the right until both arms are at shoulder height with palms facing downward. Look to the front. This is a repeat of step 3 but on the opposite side, reversing all left/right directions.

6. EXHALING

Relax the anus, relax the pelvis and relax the lower abdomen; slowly transfer the centre of gravity onto the left foot while pivoting on the ball of the right foot to push the heel away as the right leg straightens turning the upper body to face the left in a left side bow stance.

At the same time, swing the right arm upwards then downwards with fingers trailing and the left arm downwards then upwards with fingers trailing until the left Zhigou SJ-6 is firmly pressed against the right Neiguan PC-6, then hyperextend the left hand to point the fingers up and flex the right hand to point the fingers down. Look straight ahead to the left. This is a repeat of step 2.

7. INHALING

Raise the anus, tilt the pelvis and draw in the lower abdomen; pivot on the right foot and bring the heel back to its original position and turn the upper body rightward to face the front with the weight evenly distributed in a horse stance. Simultaneously, lift the right arm, lower the left arm and bring them in front of the chest in the ball holding position.

Without pausing, swing the right arm in an arc upward, outward and downward to the right while the left arm swings in an arc upward and outward to the left until both arms are at shoulder height with palms facing downward. Look to the front. This is a repeat of step 3.

8. EXHALING

Relax the anus, relax the pelvis and relax the lower abdomen; transfer the centre of gravity to the right leg and bring the left foot back to the side of the right foot. At the same time lower both arms to the sides of the body to return to the starting position.

Part 2

Repeat on right side, reversing all left/right directions.

Main points

1. The purpose of this exercise is to eliminate Fire from the Liver and to remove Liver-Qi Stagnation.

2. The mental focus during this exercise is on the acupoints Neiguan PC-6.

3. When pivoting the foot apply more pressure towards the fourth toe to activate Zuqiaoyin GB-44.

Standing Stress Relief Exercise 7: Swimming Fish Flaps Its Tail

Starting position: Stand with the feet together, weight evenly distributed, body upright and relaxed with the hands hanging down at the sides of the body. Look straight ahead. (Fig. R.1)

Part 1

1. INHALING

Raise the anus, tilt the pelvis and draw in the lower abdomen; move the centre of gravity to the right foot, bend the right leg slightly and raise the left heel while rotating the arms inward until both palms face the rear. (Fig. R.37)

Without pause, turn the body 45 degrees to the left, step out with the left foot, Daoyin Diagonal Stepping, to the left diagonal and set the heel on the ground in a toe-up empty stance. Simultaneously, swing the arms upward to the sides to shoulder height with palms still facing the rear. Look straight ahead to the left diagonal. (Fig. R.38)

Fig. R.37

Fig. R.38

2. EXHALING

Relax the anus, relax the pelvis and relax the lower abdomen; move the centre of gravity forward to the left foot into a left bow stance. At the same time, sweep the arms forward, rotating them until the palms face downward, right hand extending to the front at shoulder height, fingers pointing forward, and left hand sweeping down to the front of the upper abdomen, fingers pointing to the right. Look straight ahead to the left diagonal. (Fig. R.39)

Fig. R.39

3. INHALING

Raise the anus, tilt the pelvis and draw in the lower abdomen; straighten the left leg and transfer the centre of gravity to the bent right leg in a left toe-up empty stance. Simultaneously, turn the body slightly leftward and then back to the front as the left arm swings outward and forward in an arc up to the front to finish palm down at shoulder height while the right arm swings inward and downward in front of the upper abdomen, fingers pointing to the left. Head and eyes follow the left palm. (Fig. R.40, R.41)

Fig. R.40

Fig. R.41

4. EXHALING

Relax the anus, relax the pelvis and relax the lower abdomen; move the centre of gravity forward to the left foot into a left bow stance. At the same time, turn the body slightly rightward and then back to the front as the right arm swings outward and forward in an arc up to the front to finish palm down at shoulder height while the left arm swings inward and downward in front of the upper abdomen, fingers pointing to the right. Head and eyes follow the right palm.

5. INHALING

Raise the anus, tilt the pelvis and draw in the lower abdomen; straighten the left leg and transfer the centre of gravity to the bent right leg in a left toe-up empty stance. Simultaneously, turn the body slightly leftward and then back to the front as the left arm swings outward and forward in an arc up to the front to finish palm down at shoulder height while the right arm swings inward and downward in front of the upper abdomen, fingers pointing to the left. Head and eyes follow the left palm. This is a repeat of step 3.

6. EXHALING

Relax the anus, relax the pelvis and relax the lower abdomen; move the centre of gravity forward to the left foot into a left bow stance. At the same time, turn the body slightly rightward and then back to the front as the right arm swings outward and forward in an arc up to the front to finish palm down at shoulder height while the left arm swings inward and downward in front of the upper abdomen, fingers pointing to the right. Head and eyes follow the right palm. This is a repeat of step 4.

7. INHALING

Raise the anus, tilt the pelvis and draw in the lower abdomen; straighten the left leg and transfer the centre of gravity to the bent right leg in a left toe-up empty stance. Simultaneously, bring the right hand back to the upper abdomen until the fingers of both hands point to each other (Fig. R.42) and then extend both arms out to the sides, to finish palm down at shoulder height. The upper body and head now face the front and the eyes look straight ahead. (Fig. R.43)

Fig. R.42   Fig. R.43

8. EXHALING

Relax the anus, relax the pelvis and relax the lower abdomen; bring the left foot to the side of the right, feet together, and lower the arms down to the sides of the body returning to the starting position. Eyes look directly ahead.

Part 2

Repeat on right side, reversing all left/right directions.

Main points

1. The purpose of this exercise is to calm the mind.

2. The mental focus during this exercise is on the acupoints Laogong PC-8.

3. The circular movements of the arms in and out should be performed smoothly and lightly.

4. The acupoint Hegu LI-4 on the hand close to the body should align with Jiuwei RN-15 on the abdomen.

Standing Stress Relief Exercise 8: Sink Qi to Dantian

Starting position: Stand with the feet together, weight evenly distributed, body upright and relaxed with the hands hanging down at the sides of the body. Look straight ahead. (Fig. R.1)

Part 1 – Brushing from Head to Chest

1.1. INHALING

Raise the anus, tilt the pelvis, draw in the lower abdomen and move the centre of gravity over the balls of the feet. Simultaneously, rotate the arms outward until the palms face forward (Fig. R.44) then, without pausing, swing the arms slowly upward to the front until both palms rest on the forehead. Look straight ahead with half closed eyes. (Fig. R.45)

1.2. EXHALING

Relax the anus, relax the pelvis, relax the lower abdomen and move the centre of gravity over the heels. At the same time, rub the head with the hands from the forehead to the back of the neck (Fig. R.46) and then rub the neck from the back to the front. The hands meet in a prayer position in front of the neck and then move down the front of the chest to heart level. Look straight ahead with half closed eyes. (Fig. R.47)

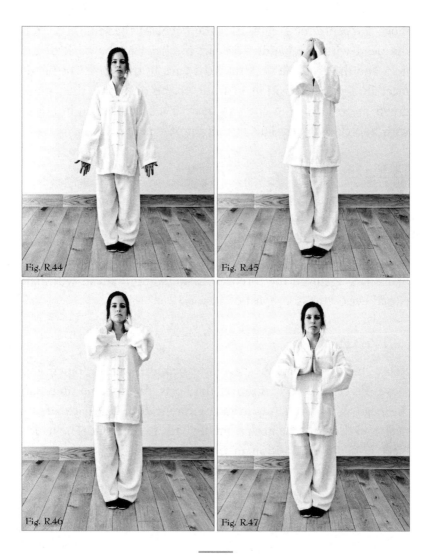

Fig. R.44

Fig. R.45

Fig. R.46

Fig. R.47

1.3. INHALING

Raise the anus, tilt the pelvis, draw in the lower abdomen and move the centre of gravity over the balls of the feet. Simultaneously, turn the fingertips to point ahead and push the arms forward, open the palms and then raise them slowly upward until both palms rest again on the forehead. Look straight ahead with half closed eyes.

1.4. EXHALING

Relax the anus, relax the pelvis, relax the lower abdomen and move the centre of gravity over the heels. At the same time, rub the head with the hands from the forehead to the back of the neck and then rub the neck from the back to the front. The hands meet in a prayer position in front of the neck and then move down the front of the chest to heart level. Look straight ahead with half closed eyes. This is a repeat of step 1.2.

1.5. INHALING

Raise the anus, tilt the pelvis, draw in the lower abdomen and move the centre of gravity over the balls of the feet. Simultaneously, turn the fingertips to point ahead and push the arms forward, open the palms and then raise them slowly upward until both palms rest again on the forehead. Look straight ahead with half closed eyes. This is a repeat of step 1.3.

1.6. EXHALING

Relax the anus, relax the pelvis, relax the lower abdomen and move the centre of gravity over the heels. At the same time, rub the head with the hands from the forehead to the back of the neck and then rub the neck from the back to the front. The hands meet in a prayer position in front of the neck and then move down the front of the chest to heart level. Look straight ahead with half closed eyes. This is a repeat of step 1.2.

1.7. INHALING

Raise the anus, tilt the pelvis, draw in the lower abdomen and move the centre of gravity over the balls of the feet. Simultaneously, turn the fingertips to point ahead and push the arms forward, open the palms and then raise them slowly upward until both palms rest again on the forehead. Look straight ahead with half closed eyes. This is a repeat of step 1.3.

1.8. EXHALING

Relax the anus, relax the pelvis, relax the lower abdomen and move the centre of gravity over the heels. At the same time, rub the head with the hands from the forehead to the back of the neck and then rub the neck from the back to the front. The hands meet in a prayer position in front of the neck and then move down the front of the chest to heart level and then continue to move down the body to both sides back into the starting position. Look straight ahead with half closed eyes.

Part 2 – Brushing from Chest to Lower Abdomen

2.1. INHALING

Raise the anus, tilt the pelvis, draw in the lower abdomen and move the centre of gravity over the balls of the feet. Simultaneously, rotate the arms inward until the palms face the rear, raise them slowly upward to shoulder height (Fig. R.48) then swing them forward while rotating them outward, finally bringing the palms together over the Middle Dantian, left palm on the inside. Look straight ahead with half closed eyes. (Fig. R.49)

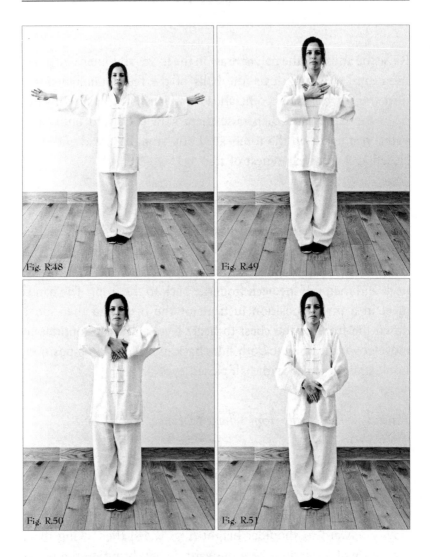

Fig. R.48 Fig. R.49 Fig. R.50 Fig. R.51

2.2. EXHALING

Relax the anus, relax the pelvis, relax the lower abdomen and move the centre of gravity over the heels. At the same time, raise the elbows, point the fingertips downward (Fig. R.50) and then move the palms downward rubbing from the Middle Dantian to the Lower Dantian. Look straight ahead with half closed eyes. (Fig. R.51)

2.3. INHALING

Raise the anus, tilt the pelvis, draw in the lower abdomen and move the centre of gravity over the balls of the feet. Simultaneously, separate the hands to the sides of the body and raise them slowly upward to shoulder height then swing them forward while rotating the arms outward, finally bringing the palms together over the Middle Dantian with the left palm on the inside. Look straight ahead with half closed eyes.

2.4. EXHALING

Relax the anus, relax the pelvis, relax the lower abdomen and move the centre of gravity over the heels. At the same time, raise the elbows, point the fingertips downward and then move the palms downward rubbing from the Middle Dantian to the Lower Dantian. Look straight ahead with half closed eyes. This is a repeat of step 2.2.

2.5. INHALING

Raise the anus, tilt the pelvis, draw in the lower abdomen and move the centre of gravity over the balls of the feet. Simultaneously, separate the hands to the sides of the body and raise them slowly upward to shoulder height then swing them forward while rotating the arms outward, finally bringing the palms together over the Middle Dantian with the left palm on the inside. Look straight ahead with half closed eyes. This is a repeat of step 2.3.

2.6. EXHALING

Relax the anus, relax the pelvis, relax the lower abdomen and move the centre of gravity over the heels. At the same time, raise the elbows up, point the fingertips downward and then move the palms downward rubbing from the Middle Dantian to the Lower Dantian. Look straight ahead with half closed eyes. This is a repeat of step 2.2.

2.7. INHALING

Raise the anus, tilt the pelvis, draw in the lower abdomen and move the centre of gravity over the balls of the feet. Simultaneously, separate the hands to the sides of the body and raise them slowly upward to shoulder height then swing them forward while rotating the arms outward, finally bringing the palms together over the Middle Dantian with the left palm on the inside. Look straight ahead with half closed eyes. This is a repeat of step 2.3.

2.8. EXHALING

Relax the anus, relax the pelvis, relax the lower abdomen and move the centre of gravity over the heels. At the same time, raise the elbows, point the fingertips downward and then move the palms downward rubbing from the Middle Dantian to the Lower Dantian. Look straight ahead with half closed eyes. This is a repeat of step 2.2.

CLOSING

Separate and raise the arms slowly upward to the sides to waist height and then swing them forward while rotating them outward and bringing the palms together over the Lower Dantian. Look straight ahead with half closed eyes.

Main points

1. The purpose of this exercise is to close the routine down and return the body, breath and mind to their normal states.

2. The mental focus during Part 1 of this exercise is on the Middle Dantian while inhaling and then changes to guiding Qi from the Upper Dantian to the Middle Dantian while exhaling. In Part 2 the mental focus is

on the Lower Dantian while inhaling and then changes to guiding Qi from the Middle Dantian to the Lower Dantian while exhaling.

3. The feet do not move during this exercise but the weight moves to the balls of the feet during inhaling and then to the heels during exhaling. In the final position the weight is evenly distributed.

4. The closing is different for men and women. During the closing men put their left hand on the Lower Dantian and cover it with their right hand while women put their right hand over the Lower Dantian and cover it with their left hand.

SEATED STRESS RELIEF ROUTINE

Seated Stress Relief Exercise 1:
Taiji Breathing

Starting position: Sit on the edge of the seat with the feet together, body upright and relaxed, hands placed on the upper thighs with fingers pointing to the knees. Look straight ahead. (Fig. RS.1)

Fig. RS.1

Recite silently:

> *In the late evening stillness leave all troubles behind,*
>
> *Set the mind on Dantian and seal the seven openings.*
>
> *Breathe gently and unhurried and raise the magpie bridge,*
>
> *With the body light as a swallow soaring through the skies.*

Part 1

1. INHALING

Raise the anus, tilt the pelvis and draw in the lower abdomen; raise the left heel and slightly separate the legs, Daoyin Side Stepping, until the left foot is in line with the left shoulder then place the heel down while rotating the left arm outward until the palm faces outward from the left side. Then repeat the actions with the right leg and right arm. When both palms face outward from the sides apply some slight pressure to the ground to put weight onto the balls of the feet and raise the arms sideways until they are over the head with the palms facing acupoint Baihui DU-20 on the crown, fingertips pointing to each other. Look straight ahead. (Fig. RS.2, RS.3)

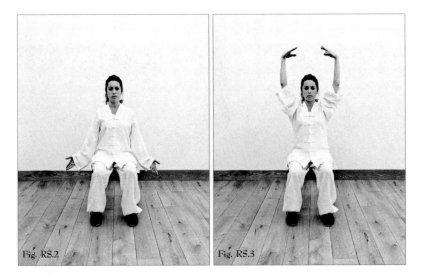

Fig. RS.2 Fig. RS.3

2. EXHALING

Relax the anus, relax the pelvis and relax the lower abdomen and change the direction of the pressure on the ground to move the weight to the heels. At the same time, lower the arms in front of the body until the hands reach the Lower Dantian with the palms facing downward. Look straight ahead. (Fig. RS.4)

Fig. RS.4

3. INHALING

Raise the anus, tilt the pelvis and draw in the lower abdomen; rotate the arms outward until both palms face out from the sides, then apply some slight pressure to the ground to put weight onto the balls of the feet while raising the arms sideways until they are over the head with the palms facing acupoint Baihui DU-20 on the crown, fingertips pointing to each other. Look straight ahead.

4. EXHALING

Relax the anus, relax the pelvis and relax the lower abdomen and change the direction of the pressure on the ground to move the weight to the heels. At the same time, lower the arms in front of the body until the hands reach the Lower Dantian with the palms facing downward. Look straight ahead. This is a repeat of step 2.

5. INHALING

Raise the anus, tilt the pelvis and draw in the lower abdomen; rotate the arms outward until both palms face out from the sides, then apply some slight pressure to the ground to put weight onto the balls of the feet while raising the arms sideways until they are over the head with the palms facing acupoint Baihui DU-20 on the crown, fingertips pointing to each other. Look straight ahead. This is a repeat of step 3.

6. EXHALING

Relax the anus, relax the pelvis and relax the lower abdomen and change the direction of the pressure on the ground to move the weight to the heels. At the same time, lower the arms in front of the body until the hands reach the Lower Dantian with the palms facing downward. Look straight ahead. This is a repeat of step 2.

7. INHALING

Raise the anus, tilt the pelvis and draw in the lower abdomen; rotate the arms outward until both palms face out from the sides, then apply some slight pressure to the ground to put weight onto the balls of the feet while raising the arms sideways until they are over the head with the palms facing acupoint Baihui DU-20 on the crown, fingertips pointing to each other. Look straight ahead. This is a repeat of step 3.

8. EXHALING

Relax the anus, relax the pelvis and relax the lower abdomen; raise the heels and bring the right foot inwards and then place the left next to it. At the same time, lower both arms down and place the hands on the thighs back in the starting position. Look straight ahead.

Part 2

Repeat, reversing all left/right directions.

Main points

1. The purpose of this exercise is to open the sequence; set the breathing, movement and mind in harmony (Three Regulations) for the rest of the routine.

2. The mental focus during this exercise is on the acupoints Laogong PC-8 on the palms of the hands while raising the arms and then changes to the Lower Dantian in the lower abdomen while lowering the arms.

3. Throughout the whole exercise, when the arms are being raised the palms become Yang palms and the weight shifts to the balls of the feet and when the arms are being lowered the palms change to Yin palms and the weight shifts to the heels.

Seated Stress Relief Exercise 2: Swirling Water

Starting position: Sit on the edge of the seat with the feet together, body upright and relaxed, hands placed on the upper thighs with fingers pointing to the knees. Look straight ahead. (Fig. RS.1)

Part 1

1. INHALING

Raise the anus, tilt the pelvis and draw in the lower abdomen; raise the left heel while moving the elbows outward and pivoting the hands until the fingertips point to each other. (Fig. RS.5)

Without pause turn the body 45 degrees to the left, step out with the left foot, Daoyin Diagonal Stepping, to the left diagonal and set the heel on the ground in a toe-up empty stance while raising the hands upwards close to the body to upper chest height, palms still facing inward. (Fig. RS.6)

2. EXHALING

Relax the anus, relax the pelvis and relax the lower abdomen; lower the left foot to the ground and apply some pressure to put weight onto the ball of the foot. At the same time, slowly extend the arms outward in an embracing position. Turn the palms slightly upward and look towards them. (Fig. RS.7)

Fig. RS.5

Fig. RS.6

Fig. RS.7

Fig. RS.8

3. INHALING

Raise the anus, tilt the pelvis and draw in the lower abdomen; pull the left foot and toes back into a toe-up empty stance. Simultaneously, turn the body rightward and swing the right arm, palm upward at shoulder height, in an arc to the rear as far as possible. Head and eyes follow the right palm. (Fig. RS.8)

4. EXHALING

Relax the anus, relax the pelvis and relax the lower abdomen; lower the left foot to the ground and apply some pressure to put weight onto the ball of the foot. At the same time, turn the body leftward, move the right hand to the side of the head, palm forward, fingers pointing left and then push the palm to the front alongside the left palm. Look towards the hands. (Fig. RS.9)

5. INHALING

Raise the anus, tilt the pelvis and draw in the lower abdomen; pull the left foot and toes back into a toe-up empty stance. Simultaneously, turn the body leftward and swing the left arm, palm upward at shoulder height, in an arc to the rear as far as possible. Head and eyes follow the left palm. This is the same as step 3 but with the left arm. (Fig. RS.10)

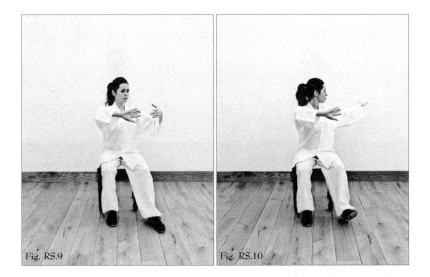

Fig. RS.9   Fig. RS.10

6. EXHALING

Relax the anus, relax the pelvis and relax the lower abdomen; lower the left foot to the ground and apply some pressure to put weight onto the ball of the foot. At the same time, turn the body rightward, move the left hand to the side of the head, palm forward, fingers pointing right and then push the palm to the front alongside the right palm. Look towards the back of the hands. This is the same as step 4 but with the left arm. (Fig. RS.11)

7. INHALING

Raise the anus, tilt the pelvis and draw in the lower abdomen; pull the left foot and toes back into a toe-up empty stance. Simultaneously, rotate both palms to face inwards and then turn the body rightward to face the front. (Fig. RS.12)

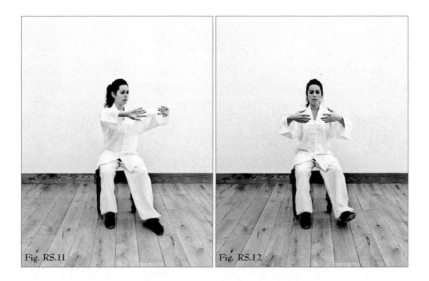

Fig. RS.11   Fig. RS.12

8. EXHALING

Relax the anus, relax the pelvis and relax the lower abdomen; bring the left foot to the side of the right, feet together, draw the palms close to the chest and lower them to the starting position.

Part 2

Repeat, reversing all left/right directions.

Main points

1. The purpose of this exercise is to calm the mind.

2. The mental focus during this exercise is on the acupoints Laogong PC-8.

3. When moving the arm to the rear, sweep it as far as possible to feel tightness over the scapula.

Seated Stress Relief Exercise 3: Eagle Soaring in the Sky

Starting position: Sit on the edge of the seat with the feet together, body upright and relaxed, hands placed on the upper thighs with fingers pointing to the knees. Look straight ahead. (Fig. RS.1)

Part 1

1. INHALING

Raise the anus, tilt the pelvis and draw in the lower abdomen; raise the left heel while both arms rotate outward until the palms face forward at the side of the thighs. (Fig. RS.13)

Without pause turn the body 45 degrees to the left, step out with the left foot, Daoyin Diagonal Stepping, to the left diagonal and set the heel on the ground in a toe-up empty stance. Slowly raise the arms upward to the front to shoulder level, hands moving towards each other until the right palm is over, but not touching, the left palm, palms facing upward. Look towards the hands. (Fig. RS.14)

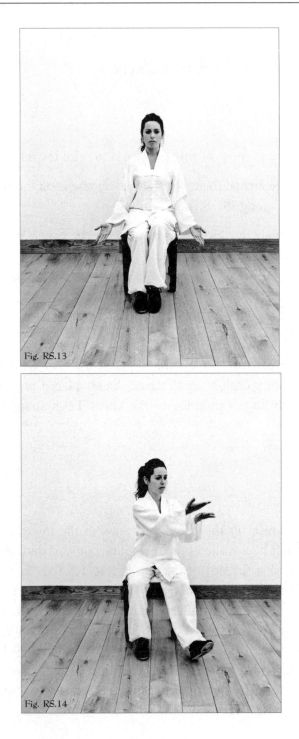

Fig. RS.13

Fig. RS.14

2. EXHALING

Relax the anus, relax the pelvis and relax the lower abdomen; rotate both legs outward while lowering the left foot, toes out, and lifting the right heel up but keeping all the toes touching the ground. Push all the toes into the ground. At the same time, turn the torso to the left, rotate the hands so that the fingertips point to the chest and then pass by the armpits to stretch the arms straight, left arm angled down and backward, right arm angled up and forward, with palms facing upward. Look at the left hand. (Fig. RS.15, RS.16)

Fig. RS.15

Fig. RS.16

3. INHALING

Raise the anus, tilt the pelvis and draw in the lower abdomen; rotate both legs inward while pulling the left foot and toes back into a toe-up empty stance and placing the right heel back in its starting position. Simultaneously, raise the left arm and lower the right arm while swinging them both to the front of the body at shoulder height with palms facing downward. The body now faces forward and the eyes look straight ahead. (Fig. RS.17)

Fig. RS.17

4. EXHALING

Relax the anus, relax the pelvis and relax the lower abdomen; bring the left foot to the side of the right, feet together, and lower the hands down the front and place them on the thighs in the starting position. Look straight ahead.

5. INHALING

Raise the anus, tilt the pelvis and draw in the lower abdomen; raise the right heel while both arms rotate outward until the palms face forward at the side of the thighs.

Without pause turn the body 45 degrees to the right, step out with the right foot, Daoyin Diagonal Stepping, to the right diagonal and set the heel on the ground in a toe-up empty stance. Slowly raise the arms upward to the front to shoulder level, hands moving towards each other until the left palm is over, but not touching, the right palm, palms facing upward. Look towards the hands. This is a repeat of step 1 with all left/right directions reversed.

6. EXHALING

Relax the anus, relax the pelvis and relax the lower abdomen; rotate both legs outward while lowering the right foot, toes out, and lifting the left heel up but keeping all the toes touching the ground. Push all the toes into the ground. At the same time, turn the torso to the right, rotate the hands so that the fingertips point to the chest and then pass by the armpits to stretch the arms straight, right arm angled down and backward, left arm angled up and forward, with palms facing upward. Look at the right hand. This is a repeat of step 2 with all left/right directions reversed.

7. INHALING

Raise the anus, tilt the pelvis and draw in the lower abdomen; rotate both legs inward while pulling the right foot and toes back into a toe-up empty stance and placing the left heel back in its starting position. Simultaneously, raise the right arm and lower the left arm while swinging them both to the front of the body at shoulder height with palms facing downward. The body now faces forward and the eyes look straight ahead. This is a repeat of step 3 with all left/right directions reversed.

8. EXHALING

Relax the anus, relax the pelvis and relax the lower abdomen; bring the right foot to the side of the left, feet together, and lower the hands down the front and place them on the thighs in the starting position. This is a repeat of step 4 with all left/right directions reversed.

Part 2

Repeat.

Main points

1. The purpose of this exercise is to eliminate Fire from the Heart and Liver and to dispel Phlegm.

2. The mental focus during this exercise is on the acupoint Mingmen DU-4.

3. When rotating the arms twist them as much as possible.

Seated Stress Relief Exercise 4: Black Dragon Displays Talons

Starting position: Sit on the edge of the seat with the feet together, body upright and relaxed, hands placed on the upper thighs with fingers pointing to the knees. Look straight ahead. (Fig. RS.1)

Part 1

1. INHALING

Raise the anus, tilt the pelvis and draw in the lower abdomen; raise the left heel and slightly separate the legs, Daoyin Side Stepping, until the left foot is in line with the left shoulder then place the heel down while swinging the arms out to the sides with both palms facing the rear. Without pause raise the arms sideways up to shoulder level and then rotate them until the palms face downward. Look to the left. (Fig. RS.18, RS.19)

Fig. RS.18

2. EXHALING

Relax the anus, relax the pelvis and relax the lower abdomen; raise the right leg and cross it over the left thigh with the right foot close to the left knee, Daoyin Cross-over Stepping. At the same time, swing the arms, at shoulder height, in front of the body with palms facing downward. Body, arms and head all face the left diagonal. (Fig. RS.20)

Fig. RS.19

Fig. RS.20

Without pause draw the hands back and down until the right palm is resting on the right thigh at Jimen SP-11 and the left thumb is touching the right foot at Xingjian LR-2 acupoint. The movement concludes with the right side of the chest expanding while the left side contracts and the left thumb presses firmly on acupoint Xingjian LR-2. Look at the right foot. (Fig. RS.21)

Fig. RS.21

3. INHALING

Raise the anus, tilt the pelvis and draw in the lower abdomen; move both hands upward, close to the chest, to shoulder height and then stretch the fingers wide while pushing the arms to the left diagonal. Look towards the hands. (Fig. RS.22)

Fig. RS.22

4. EXHALING

Relax the anus, relax the pelvis and relax the lower abdomen; draw the hands back and down until the right palm is resting on the right thigh at Jimen SP-11 and the left thumb is touching the right foot at Xingjian LR-2 acupoint. The movement concludes with the right side of the chest expanding while the left side contracts and the left thumb presses firmly on acupoint Xingjian LR-2. Look at the right foot.

5. INHALING

Raise the anus, tilt the pelvis and draw in the lower abdomen; move both hands upward, close to the chest, to shoulder height and then stretch the fingers wide while pushing the arms to the left diagonal. Look towards the hands. This is a repeat of step 3.

6. EXHALING

Relax the anus, relax the pelvis and relax the lower abdomen; draw the hands back and down until the right palm is resting on the right thigh at Jimen SP-11 and the left thumb is touching the right foot at Xingjian LR-2 acupoint. The movement concludes with the right side of the chest expanding while the left side contracts and the left thumb presses firmly on acupoint Xingjian LR-2. Look at the right foot. This is a repeat of step 4.

7. INHALING

Raise the anus, tilt the pelvis and draw in the lower abdomen; move both hands upward, close to the chest, to shoulder height, palm down with the fingers pointing at each other.

Without pause place the right foot back on the ground as in step 1. The arms, meanwhile, spread out to the sides at shoulder height palms down and the head and eyes look towards the right hand. (Fig. RS.23, RS.24)

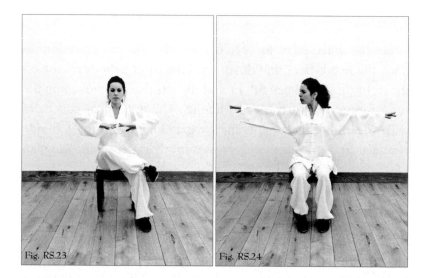

Fig. RS.23   Fig. RS.24

8. EXHALING

Relax the anus, relax the pelvis and relax the lower abdomen; bring the left foot to the side of the right, feet together, and lower the hands down to the thighs returning to the starting position. Eyes look directly ahead.

Part 2

Repeat, reversing all left/right directions.

Main points

1. The purpose of this exercise is to eliminate Fire from the Liver and to remove Liver-Qi Stagnation.

2. The mental focus during this exercise is on the acupoints Xingjian LR-2.

3. When spreading the fingers stretch them as far apart as possible.

4. Jimen SP-11 is a point of reference not a point of focus.

Seated Stress Relief Exercise 5: Dragon Hiding in the Blue Sea

Starting position: Sit on the edge of the seat with the feet together, body upright and relaxed, hands placed on the upper thighs with fingers pointing to the knees. Look straight ahead. (Fig. RS.1)

Part 1

1. INHALING

Raise the anus, tilt the pelvis and draw in the lower abdomen; raise the left heel and slightly separate the legs, Daoyin Side Stepping, until the left foot is in line with the left shoulder then place the heel down while rotating the arms outward until both palms face forward. Without pause raise the arms upward to the front to shoulder level, hands moving towards each other until the right palm is resting on the top of the left palm. Look straight ahead. (Fig. RS.25, RS.26)

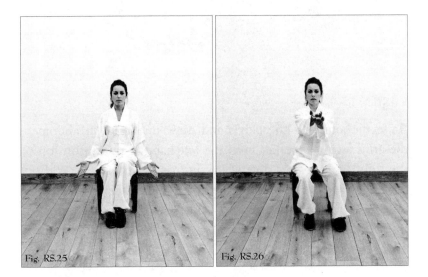

Fig. RS.25   Fig. RS.26

2. EXHALING

Relax the anus, relax the pelvis and relax the lower abdomen; raise the left leg and cross it over the right thigh with the left foot close to the right knee, Daoyin Cross-over Stepping. At the same time, curl the arms in toward the chest and turn the palms over to face downward. Then push the right palm down and out to the right side while the left arm rotates and pushes up and to the left. Look to the right. (Fig. RS.27, RS.28)

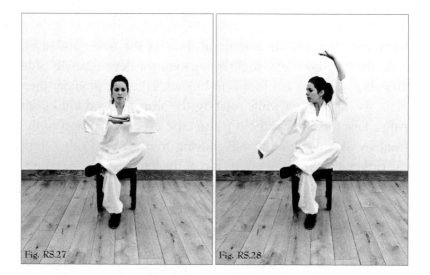

Fig. RS.27   Fig. RS.28

3. INHALING

Raise the anus, tilt the pelvis and draw in the lower abdomen; the arms swing together until the left hand is resting on top of the right hand, palms downward, in front of the chest. Without pausing, place the left foot back on the ground; keeping the hands together turn the palms upward while straightening the arms out to the front. Look straight ahead.

4. EXHALING

Relax the anus, relax the pelvis and relax the lower abdomen; bring the left foot to the side of the right foot and at the same time separate the hands and turn them palm down. Then lower both hands to the thighs back in the starting position. Look straight ahead.

5. INHALING

Raise the anus, tilt the pelvis and draw in the lower abdomen; raise the right heel and slightly separate the legs, Daoyin Side Stepping, until the right foot is in line with the right shoulder then place the heel down while rotating the arms outward until both palms face forward. Without pause raise the arms upward to the front to shoulder level, hands moving towards each other until the left palm is resting on the top of the right palm. Look straight ahead. This is a repeat of step 1 with all left/right directions reversed.

6. EXHALING

Relax the anus, relax the pelvis and relax the lower abdomen; raise the right leg and cross it over the left thigh with the right foot close to the left knee, Daoyin Cross-over Stepping. At the same time, curl the arms in toward the chest and turn the palms over to face downward. Then push the left palm down and out to the left side while the right arm rotates and pushes up and to the right. Look to the left. This is a repeat of step 2 with all left/right directions reversed.

7. INHALING

Raise the anus, tilt the pelvis and draw in the lower abdomen; the arms swing together until the right hand is resting on top of the left hand, palms downward, in front of the chest. Without pausing, place the right foot back on the ground; keeping the hands together turn the palms upward while straightening the arms out to the front. Look straight ahead. This is a repeat of step 3 with all left/right directions reversed.

8. EXHALING

Relax the anus, relax the pelvis and relax the lower abdomen; bring the right foot to the side of the left foot and at the same time separate the hands and turn them palm down. Then lower both hands to the thighs back in the starting position. Look straight ahead. This is a repeat of step 4 with all left/right directions reversed.

Part 2

Repeat.

Main points

1. The purpose of this exercise is to eliminate Fire from the Heart and Liver and to dispel Phlegm.

2. The mental focus during this exercise is on the acupoints Laogong PC-8.

Seated Stress Relief Exercise 6: Swirling Clouds

Starting position: Sit on the edge of the seat with the feet together, body upright and relaxed, hands placed on the upper thighs with fingers pointing to the knees. Look straight ahead. (Fig. RS.1)

Part 1

1. INHALING

Raise the anus, tilt the pelvis and draw in the lower abdomen; raise the left heel and slightly separate the legs, Daoyin Side Stepping, until the left foot is in line with the left shoulder then place the heel down while moving the left arm out to the side and bending the wrist so that the fingertips are pointing to the hips. Then repeat the actions with the right leg and right arm. Without pause raise the arms sideways until they are at shoulder level with the palms facing down. Look straight ahead. (Fig. RS.29, RS.30)

2. EXHALING

Relax the anus, relax the pelvis and relax the lower abdomen; pivot on the ball of the right foot to push the heel to the right, then lift the heel to apply pressure to the toes and turn the upper body to face the left. At the same time, swing the right arm upwards then downwards with fingers trailing and the left arm downwards then upwards with fingers trailing until the left Zhigou SJ-6 is firmly pressed against the right Neiguan

Fig. RS.29

Fig. RS.30

Fig. RS.31

PC-6, then hyperextend the left hand to point the fingers up and flex the right hand to point the fingers down. Look straight ahead to the left. (Fig. RS.31)

Fig. RS.32

Fig. RS.33

3. INHALING

Raise the anus, tilt the pelvis and draw in the lower abdomen; pivot on the right foot and bring the heel back to the ground and turn the upper body rightward to face the front with the weight on the heels. Simultaneously, lift the right arm, lower the left arm and bring them in front of the chest in a ball holding position. Without pausing, swing the right arm in an arc upward, outward and downward to the right while the left arm swings in an arc upward and outward to the left until both arms are at shoulder height with palms facing downward. Look to the front. (Fig. RS.32, RS.33)

4. EXHALING

Relax the anus, relax the pelvis and relax the lower abdomen; pivot on the ball of the left foot to push the heel to the left, then lift the heel to apply pressure to the toes and turn the upper body to face the right. At the same time, swing the left arm upwards then downwards with fingers trailing and the right arm downwards then upwards with fingers trailing until the right Zhigou SJ-6 is firmly pressed against the left Neiguan PC-6, then hyperextend the right hand to point the fingers up and flex the left hand to point the fingers down. Look straight ahead to the right. This is a repeat of step 2 with all left/right directions reversed.

5. INHALING

Raise the anus, tilt the pelvis and draw in the lower abdomen; pivot on the left foot and bring the heel back to the ground and turn the upper body leftward to face the front with the weight on the heels. Simultaneously, lift the left arm, lower the right arm and bring them in front of the chest in a ball holding position. Without pausing, swing the left arm in an arc upward, outward and downward to the left while the right arm swings in an arc upward and outward to the right until both arms are at shoulder height with palms facing downward. Look to the front. This is a repeat of step 3 with all left/right directions reversed.

6. EXHALING

Relax the anus, relax the pelvis and relax the lower abdomen; pivot on the ball of the right foot to push the heel to the right, then lift the heel to apply pressure to the toes and turn the upper body to face the left. At the same time, swing the right arm upwards then downwards with fingers trailing and the left arm downwards then upwards with fingers trailing until the left Zhigou SJ-6 is firmly pressed against the right Neiguan PC-6, then hyperextend the left hand to point the fingers up and flex the right hand to point the fingers down. Look straight ahead to the left.

7. INHALING

Raise the anus, tilt the pelvis and draw in the lower abdomen; pivot on the right foot and bring the heel back to the ground and turn the upper body rightward to face the front with the weight on the heels. Simultaneously, lift the right arm, lower the left arm and bring them in front of the chest in a ball holding position. Without pausing, swing the right arm in an arc upward, outward and downward to the right while the left arm swings in an arc upward and outward to the left until both arms are at shoulder height with palms facing downward. Look to the front.

8. EXHALING

Relax the anus, relax the pelvis and relax the lower abdomen; raise the heels and bring the right foot inwards and then place the left next to it. At the same time, sweep both arms down and place the hands on the thighs back in the starting position. Look straight ahead.

Part 2

Repeat, reversing all left/right directions.

Main points

1. The purpose of this exercise is to eliminate Fire from the Liver and to remove Liver-Qi Stagnation.

2. The mental focus during this exercise is on the acupoints Neiguan PC-6.

3. When pivoting the foot apply more pressure towards the fourth toe to activate Zuqiaoyin GB-44.

Seated Stress Relief Exercise 7: Swimming Fish Flaps Its Tail

Starting position: Sit on the edge of the seat with the feet together, body upright and relaxed, hands placed on the upper thighs with fingers pointing to the knees. Look straight ahead. (Fig. RS.1)

Part 1

1. INHALING

Raise the anus, tilt the pelvis and draw in the lower abdomen; raise the left heel while swinging the arms out to the sides with both palms facing the rear. (Fig. RS.34)

Fig. RS.34

Without pause turn the body 45 degrees to the left, step out with the left foot, Daoyin Diagonal Stepping, to the left diagonal and set the heel on the ground in a toe-up empty stance. Simultaneously, swing the arms upward to the sides to shoulder height with palms still facing the rear. Look straight ahead to the left diagonal. (Fig. RS.35)

2. EXHALING

Relax the anus, relax the pelvis and relax the lower abdomen; lower the left foot to the ground and apply some pressure to put weight onto the ball of the foot. At the same time, sweep the arms forward, rotating them until the palms face downward, right hand extending to the front at shoulder height, fingers pointing forward, and left hand sweeping down to the front of the upper abdomen, fingers pointing to the right. Look straight ahead to the left diagonal. (Fig. RS.36)

Fig. RS.35

Fig. RS.36

3. INHALING

Raise the anus, tilt the pelvis and draw in the lower abdomen; pull the left foot and toes back into a toe-up empty stance. Simultaneously, turn the body slightly leftward and then back to the front as the left arm swings outward and forward in an arc up to the front to finish palm down at shoulder height while the right arm swings inward and downward in front of the upper abdomen, fingers pointing to the left. Head and eyes follow the left palm. (Fig. RS.37)

Fig. RS.37

4. EXHALING

Relax the anus, relax the pelvis and relax the lower abdomen; lower the left foot to the ground and apply some pressure to put weight onto the ball of the foot. At the same time, turn the body slightly rightward and then back to the front as the right arm swings outward and forward in an arc up to the front to finish palm down at shoulder height while the left arm swings inward and downward in front of the upper abdomen, fingers pointing to the right. Head and eyes follow the right palm.

5. INHALING

Raise the anus, tilt the pelvis and draw in the lower abdomen; pull the left foot and toes back into a toe-up empty stance. Simultaneously, turn the body slightly leftward and then back to the front as the left arm swings outward and forward in an arc up to the front to finish palm down at shoulder height while the right arm swings inward and downward in front of the upper abdomen, fingers pointing to the left. Head and eyes follow the left palm. This is a repeat of step 3.

6. EXHALING

Relax the anus, relax the pelvis and relax the lower abdomen; lower the left foot to the ground and apply some pressure to put weight onto the ball of the foot. At the same time, turn the body slightly rightward and then back to the front as the right arm swings outward and forward in an arc up to the front to finish palm down at shoulder height while the left arm swings inward and downward in front of the upper abdomen, fingers pointing to the right. Head and eyes follow the right palm. This is a repeat of step 4.

7. INHALING

Raise the anus, tilt the pelvis and draw in the lower abdomen; pull the left foot and toes back into a toe-up empty stance. Simultaneously, bring the right hand back to the upper abdomen until the fingers of both hands point to each other and then extend both arms out to the sides, to finish palm down at shoulder height. The upper body and head now face the front and the eyes look straight ahead. (Fig. RS.38, RS.39)

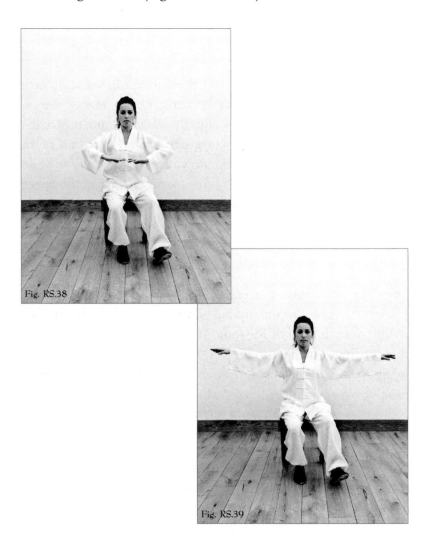

Fig. RS.38

Fig. RS.39

8. EXHALING

Relax the anus, relax the pelvis and relax the lower abdomen; bring the left foot to the side of the right, feet together, and lower the hands down to the thighs returning to the starting position. Eyes look directly ahead.

Part 2

Repeat, reversing all left/right directions.

Main points

1. The purpose of this exercise is to calm the mind.

2. The mental focus during this exercise is on the acupoints Laogong PC-8.

3. The circular movements of the arms in and out should be performed smoothly and lightly.

4. The acupoint Hegu LI-4 on the hand close to the body should align with Jiuwei RN-15 on the abdomen.

Seated Stress Relief Exercise 8:
Sink Qi to Dantian

Starting position: Sit on the edge of the seat with the feet together, body upright and relaxed, hands placed on the upper thighs with fingers pointing to the knees. Look straight ahead. (Fig. RS.1)

Part 1 – Brushing from Head to Chest

1.1. INHALING

Raise the anus, tilt the pelvis, draw in the lower abdomen and move the centre of gravity over the balls of the feet. Simultaneously, rotate the arms outward until the palms face forward then, without pausing, swing the arms slowly upward to the front until both palms rest on the forehead. Look straight ahead with half closed eyes. (Fig. RS.40)

Fig. RS.40

1.2. EXHALING

Relax the anus, relax the pelvis, relax the lower abdomen and move the centre of gravity over the heels. At the same time, rub the head with the hands from the forehead to the back of the neck and then rub the neck from the back to the front. The hands meet in a prayer position in front of the neck and then move down the front of the chest to heart level. Look straight ahead with half closed eyes. (Fig. RS.41)

Fig. RS.41

1.3. INHALING

Raise the anus, tilt the pelvis, draw in the lower abdomen and move the centre of gravity over the balls of the feet. Simultaneously, turn the fingertips to point ahead and push the arms forward, open the palms and then raise them slowly upward until both palms rest again on the forehead. Look straight ahead with half closed eyes.

1.4. EXHALING

Relax the anus, relax the pelvis, relax the lower abdomen and move the centre of gravity over the heels. At the same time, rub the head with the hands from the forehead to the back of the neck and then rub the neck from the back to the front. The hands meet in a prayer position in front of the neck and then move down the front of the chest to heart level. Look straight ahead with half closed eyes. This is a repeat of step 1.2.

1.5. INHALING

Raise the anus, tilt the pelvis, draw in the lower abdomen and move the centre of gravity over the balls of the feet. Simultaneously, turn the fingertips to point ahead and push the arms forward, open the palms and then raise them slowly upward until both palms rest again on the forehead. Look straight ahead with half closed eyes. This is a repeat of step 1.3.

1.6. EXHALING

Relax the anus, relax the pelvis, relax the lower abdomen and move the centre of gravity over the heels. At the same time, rub the head with the hands from the forehead to the back of the neck and then rub the neck from the back to the front. The hands meet in a prayer position in front of the neck and then move down the front of the chest to heart level. Look straight ahead with half closed eyes. This is a repeat of step 1.2.

1.7. INHALING

Raise the anus, tilt the pelvis, draw in the lower abdomen and move the centre of gravity over the balls of the feet. Simultaneously, turn the fingertips to point ahead and push the arms forward, open the palms and then raise them slowly upward until both palms rest again on the forehead. Look straight ahead with half closed eyes. This is a repeat of step 1.3.

1.8. EXHALING

Relax the anus, relax the pelvis, relax the lower abdomen and move the centre of gravity over the heels. At the same time, rub the head with the hands from the forehead to the back of the neck and then rub the neck from the back to the front. The hands meet in a prayer position in front of the neck and then move down the front of the chest to heart level and then continue to move down the body back into the starting position. Look straight ahead with half closed eyes.

Part 2 – Brushing from Chest to Lower Abdomen

2.1. INHALING

Raise the anus, tilt the pelvis, draw in the lower abdomen and move the centre of gravity over the balls of the feet. Simultaneously, swing the arms outward and slowly upward to the sides then swing them forward while rotating them outward, finally bringing the palms together over the Middle Dantian, left palm on the inside. Look straight ahead with half closed eyes. (Fig. RS.42)

Fig. RS.42

2.2. EXHALING

Relax the anus, relax the pelvis, relax the lower abdomen and move the centre of gravity over the heels. At the same time, raise the elbows up, point the fingertips downward and then move the palms downward rubbing from the Middle Dantian to the Lower Dantian. Look straight ahead with half closed eyes. (Fig. RS.43)

Fig. RS.43

2.3. INHALING

Raise the anus, tilt the pelvis, draw in the lower abdomen and move the centre of gravity over the balls of the feet. Simultaneously, separate the hands to the sides of the body and raise them slowly upward to shoulder height then swing them forward while rotating the arms outward, finally bringing the palms together over the Middle Dantian with the left palm on the inside. Look straight ahead with half closed eyes.

2.4. EXHALING

Relax the anus, relax the pelvis, relax the lower abdomen and move the centre of gravity over the heels. At the same time, raise the elbows up, point the fingertips downward and then move the palms downward rubbing from the Middle Dantian to the Lower Dantian. Look straight ahead with half closed eyes. This is a repeat of step 2.2.

2.5. INHALING

Raise the anus, tilt the pelvis, draw in the lower abdomen and move the centre of gravity over the balls of the feet. Simultaneously, separate the hands to the sides of the body and raise them slowly upward to shoulder height then swing them forward while rotating the arms outward, finally bringing the palms together over the Middle Dantian with the left palm on the inside. Look straight ahead with half closed eyes. This is a repeat of step 2.3.

2.6. EXHALING

Relax the anus, relax the pelvis, relax the lower abdomen and move the centre of gravity over the heels. At the same time, raise the elbows up, point the fingertips downward and then move the palms downward rubbing from the Middle Dantian to the Lower Dantian. Look straight ahead with half closed eyes. This is a repeat of step 2.2.

2.7. INHALING

Raise the anus, tilt the pelvis, draw in the lower abdomen and move the centre of gravity over the balls of the feet. Simultaneously, separate the hands to the sides of the body and raise them slowly upward to shoulder height then swing them forward while rotating the arms outward, finally bringing the palms together over the Middle Dantian with the left palm on the inside. Look straight ahead with half closed eyes. This is a repeat of step 2.3.

2.8. EXHALING

Relax the anus, relax the pelvis, relax the lower abdomen and move the centre of gravity over the heels. At the same time, raise the elbows up, point the fingertips downward and then move the palms downward rubbing from the Middle Dantian to the Lower Dantian. Look straight ahead with half closed eyes. This is a repeat of step 2.2.

CLOSING

Separate and raise the arms slowly upward to the sides to waist height and then swing them forward while rotating them outward and bringing the palms together over the Lower Dantian. Look straight ahead with half closed eyes.

Main points

1. The purpose of this exercise is to close the routine down and return the body, breath and mind to their normal state.

2. The mental focus during Part 1 of this exercise is on the Middle Dantian while inhaling and then changes to guiding Qi from the Upper Dantian to the Middle Dantian while exhaling. In Part 2 the mental focus is

on the Lower Dantian while inhaling and then changes to guiding Qi from the Middle Dantian to the Lower Dantian while exhaling.

3.   The feet do not move during this exercise but the weight moves to the balls of the feet during inhaling and then to the heels during exhaling. In the final position the weight is evenly distributed.

4.   The closing is different for men and women. During the closing men put their left hand on the Lower Dantian and cover it with their right hand while women put their right hand over the Lower Dantian and cover it with their left hand.

STANDING STRESS PREVENTION ROUTINE

The Stress Prevention routine is the Yin half of the Daoyin Stress Reduction method. Being Yin means that it is less physically demanding than the Yang Stress Relief routine because it is designed to work with stage 1 of the stress response, the "onset" and mental reaction to the stressor.

Standing Stress Prevention Exercise 1: Taiji Breathing

See the Standing Stress Relief routine for details of this exercise as it is exactly the same (pp.36–41).

Standing Stress Prevention Exercise 2: Round Fan Covers the Moon

Starting position: Stand with the feet together, weight evenly distributed, body upright and relaxed with the hands hanging down at the sides of the body. Look straight ahead. (Fig. P.1)

Fig. P.1

Part 1

1. INHALING

Raise the anus, tilt the pelvis and draw in the lower abdomen; move the centre of gravity to the right foot, bend the right leg slightly and raise the left heel while rotating the arms inward and bringing them in front of the body until the backs of the hands touch each other. (Fig. P.2)

Fig. P.2

Without pause, raise the hands up the centreline of the body to chest height, rolling them until the fingernails are pressed against each other. (Fig. P.3) Then, flick the fingers apart, separate the hands to each side of the body while stepping with the left foot out to the side, Daoyin Side Stepping, transfer the centre of gravity to the bent left leg and straighten the right leg into a left horizontal stance. Look at the left hand. (Fig. P.4)

Fig. P.3

2. EXHALING

Relax the anus, relax the pelvis and relax the lower abdomen; move the right foot across to the left behind and beyond the left foot, Daoyin Cross-over Stepping into a high cross stance. Change the

Fig. P.4

closed palms into open palms and swing the arms up in a leftward arc, hands close to each other, above the head and twist the body to face the left. Straighten the legs but keep most of the bodyweight on the left foot and look up between the hands. (Fig. P.5, P.6)

Fig. P5   Fig. P6

3. INHALING

Raise the anus, tilt the pelvis and draw in the lower abdomen; bend the legs slightly, close the palms and lower the arms to shoulder height still at the left side, (Fig. P.7) then move the right foot back to its original position on the right, straighten the left leg and transfer the centre of gravity to the bent right leg while swinging the arms horizontally to the front. Look to the front beyond the hands. (Fig. P.8)

Fig. P.7   Fig. P.8

4. EXHALING

Relax the anus, relax the pelvis and relax the lower abdomen; bring the left foot to the side of the right foot, knees still bent, while sinking the elbows. Then, slowly straighten the legs while the arms sweep down the front until the body is back in the original starting position.

5. INHALING

Raise the anus, tilt the pelvis and draw in the lower abdomen; move the centre of gravity to the left foot, bend the left leg slightly and raise the right heel while rotating the arms inward and bringing them in front of the body until the backs of the hands touch each other.

Without pause, raise the hands up the centreline of the body to chest height, rolling them until the fingernails are pressed against each other. Then, flick the fingers apart, separate the hands to each side of the body while stepping with the right foot out to the side, Daoyin Side Stepping, transfer the centre of gravity to the bent right leg and straighten the left leg into a right horizontal stance. Look at the right hand. This is the same as step 1 but in the opposite direction.

6. EXHALING

Relax the anus, relax the pelvis and relax the lower abdomen; move the left foot across to the right behind and beyond the right foot, Daoyin Cross-over Stepping into a high cross stance. Change the closed palms into open palms and swing the arms up in a rightward arc, hands close to each other, above the head and twist the body to face the right. Straighten the legs but keep most of the bodyweight on the right leg and look up between the hands. This is the same as step 2 but in the opposite direction.

7. INHALING

Raise the anus, tilt the pelvis and draw in the lower abdomen; bend the legs slightly, close the palms and lower the arms to shoulder height still at the right side, then move the left foot back to its original position on the left, straighten the right leg and transfer the centre of gravity to the bent left leg while swinging the arms horizontally to the front. Look to the front beyond the hands. This is the same as step 3 but in the opposite direction.

8. EXHALING

Relax the anus, relax the pelvis and relax the lower abdomen; bring the right foot to the side of the left foot, knees still bent, while sinking the elbows. Then, slowly straighten the legs while the arms sweep down the front until the body is back in the original starting position. This is the same as step 4 but in the opposite direction.

Part 2

This is a repeat of Part 1.

Main points

1. The purpose of this exercise is to enhance the Kidney functions so as to maintain the equilibrium of the Heart functions (in the Five Element theory this is called Water controls Fire).

2. The mental focus during this exercise is on the acupoint Mingmen DU-4.

3. When flicking the fingers apart they should make an audible sound.

4. Turn the waist fully when twisting the body to the side.

Standing Stress Prevention Exercise 3: Buffalo Ploughs the Land

Starting position: Stand with the feet together, weight evenly distributed, body upright and relaxed with the hands hanging down at the sides of the body. Look straight ahead. (Fig. P.1)

Part 1

1. INHALING

Raise the anus, tilt the pelvis and draw in the lower abdomen; move the centre of gravity to the right foot, bend the right leg slightly and raise the left heel while rotating the arms outward until the palms face forward. (Fig. P.9)

Fig. P.9

Fig. P.10

Fig. P.11•

Fig. P.12

Without pause, turn the body 45 degrees to the left, step out with the left foot, Daoyin Diagonal Stepping, to the left diagonal and set the heel on the ground in a toe-up empty stance. (Fig. P.10) Then slowly transfer the weight to the left foot while straightening the right leg into a left bow stance. Simultaneously, both arms sweep, palm up, vertically upward in front of the body to shoulder height. Look straight ahead beyond the hands. (Fig. P.11)

2. EXHALING

Relax the anus, relax the pelvis and relax the lower abdomen; straighten the left leg and transfer the centre of gravity to the bent right leg in a left toe-up empty stance. At the same time, turn the fingers inward until the fingertips point to the chest and then draw the hands to the chest while rotating both arms inward. (Fig. P.12) When the backs of the hands face each other, with the fingertips pointing down, turn the body to face the front and lower the arms, lightly brushing the body with the tigermouth area of the dragon hand until the arms are fully extended and the hands rest on the centreline of the thighs. Look straight ahead. (Fig. P.13)

Fig. P.13

3. INHALING

Raise the anus, tilt the pelvis and draw in the lower abdomen; turn the body 45 degrees to the left, straighten the right leg and transfer the centre of gravity to the left foot into a left bow stance. Simultaneously, rotate the arms outward, palms facing forward, then sweep them upward in front of the body to shoulder height. Look straight ahead beyond the hands.

4. EXHALING

Relax the anus, relax the pelvis and relax the lower abdomen; straighten the left leg and transfer the centre of gravity to the bent right leg in a left toe-up empty stance. At the same time, turn the fingers inward until the fingertips point to the chest and then draw the hands to the chest while rotating both arms inward. When the backs of the hands face each other, with the fingertips pointing down, turn the body to face the front and lower the arms, lightly brushing the body with the tigermouth area of the dragon hand until the arms are fully extended and the hands rest on the centreline of the thighs. Look straight ahead. This is a repeat of step 2.

5. INHALING

Raise the anus, tilt the pelvis and draw in the lower abdomen; turn the body 45 degrees to the left, straighten the right leg and transfer the centre of gravity to the left foot into a left bow stance. Simultaneously, rotate the arms outward, palms facing forward, then sweep them upward in front of the body to shoulder height. Look straight ahead beyond the hands. This is a repeat of step 3.

6. EXHALING

Relax the anus, relax the pelvis and relax the lower abdomen; straighten the left leg and transfer the centre of gravity to the bent right leg in a left toe-up empty stance. At the same time, turn the fingers inward until the fingertips point to the chest and then draw the hands to the chest while rotating both arms inward. When the backs of the hands face each other, with the fingertips pointing down, turn the body to face the front and lower the arms, lightly brushing the body with the tigermouth area of the dragon hand until the arms are fully extended and the hands rest on the centreline of the thighs. Look straight ahead. This is a repeat of step 2.

7. INHALING

Raise the anus, tilt the pelvis and draw in the lower abdomen; turn the body 45 degrees to the left, straighten the right leg and transfer the centre of gravity to the left foot into a left bow stance. Simultaneously, rotate the arms outward, palms facing forward, then sweep them upward in front of the body to shoulder height. Look straight ahead beyond the hands. This is a repeat of step 3.

8. EXHALING

Relax the anus, relax the pelvis and relax the lower abdomen; straighten the left leg and transfer the centre of gravity to the bent right leg in a left toe-up empty stance. At the same time turn the fingers inward until the fingertips point to the chest and then draw the hands to the chest while rotating both arms inward.

When the backs of the hands face each other, with the fingertips pointing down, turn the body to face the front, bring the left foot back to the side of the right foot, straighten the legs and lower the arms, lightly brushing the body with the tigermouth area of the dragon hand until the arms are fully extended and the hands rest on the centreline of the thighs. Finally, rotate the arms outward until the body is now in the original starting position. Look straight ahead.

Part 2

Repeat on right side, reversing all left/right directions.

Main points

1. The purpose of this exercise is to enhance the Heart functions so as to maintain the equilibrium of the Lung functions (in the Five Element theory this is called Fire controls Metal).

2. The mental focus during this exercise is on the acupoints Laogong PC-8.

3. When raising the arms to the front, rotate the arms outward and raise the little finger edge of the palm the highest.

Standing Stress Prevention Exercise 4: Distinguished Lord Combs Hair

Starting position: Stand with the feet together, weight evenly distributed, body upright and relaxed with the hands hanging down at the sides of the body. Look straight ahead. (Fig. P.1)

Part 1

1. INHALING

Raise the anus, tilt the pelvis and draw in the lower abdomen; move the centre of gravity to the right foot, bend the right leg slightly and raise the left heel while rotating the arms inward until both closed palms face the rear. (Fig. P.14)

Without pause, take a step with the left foot to the left, Daoyin Side Stepping, so that the feet are approximately twice the width of the shoulders apart; move the centre of gravity to a position between both feet and then slowly straighten the legs. Simultaneously, push both arms backward, outward and upward while turning the body slightly to the left. (Fig. P.15) When the arms reach shoulder height, rotate the arms outward until the palms face forward.

Continuing, the left arm now bends and the left closed palm is placed on the back of the head. At the same time, the right arm swings leftward across the body and the right closed palm is placed against the left jaw line. Look to the left side. (Fig. P.16)

2. EXHALING

Relax the anus, relax the pelvis and relax the lower abdomen; without moving the feet turn the body to face forward and half squat on the heels in a horse stance. At the same time, draw the right elbow to the rear, sweeping the right closed palm off the face and stopping when the palm is face up at the right side of the ribs. Meanwhile, the left elbow swings to the front allowing the left palm to brush the hair, then the arm extends forward in front of the body at shoulder height with the left closed palm changing into an eight character palm. Look at the eight character palm. (Fig. P.17)

Fig. P.14

Fig. P.15

Fig. P.16

Fig. P.17

3. INHALING

Raise the anus, tilt the pelvis and draw in the lower abdomen; without moving the feet slowly straighten the legs. Simultaneously, turn the body slightly to the right, change the left eight character palm into a closed palm and sweep it rightward across the body and place it against the right jaw line. Meanwhile, the right closed palm moves in a circular sweep, downward, backward and upward and is placed on the back of the head. Look to the right side.

4. EXHALING

Relax the anus, relax the pelvis and relax the lower abdomen; without moving the feet turn the body to face forward and half squat on the heels in a horse stance. At the same time, draw the left elbow to the rear, sweeping the left closed palm off the face and stopping when the palm is face up at the left side of the ribs. Meanwhile, the right elbow swings to the front allowing the right palm to brush the hair, then the arm extends forward in front of the body at shoulder height with the right closed palm changing into an eight character palm. Look at the eight character palm.

5. INHALING

Raise the anus, tilt the pelvis and draw in the lower abdomen; without moving the feet slowly straighten the legs. Simultaneously, turn the body slightly to the left, change the right eight character palm into a closed palm and sweep it leftward across the body and place it against the left jaw line. Meanwhile, the left closed palm moves in a circular sweep, downward, backward and upward and is placed on the back of the head. Look to the left side.

6. EXHALING

Relax the anus, relax the pelvis and relax the lower abdomen; without moving the feet turn the body to face forward and half squat on the heels in a horse stance. At the same time, draw the right elbow to the rear, sweeping the right closed palm off the face and stopping when the palm is face up at the right side of the ribs. Meanwhile, the left elbow swings to the front allowing the left palm to brush the hair, then the arm extends forward in front of the body at shoulder height with the left closed palm changing into an eight character palm. Look at the eight character palm. This is a repeat of step 2.

7. INHALING

Raise the anus, tilt the pelvis and draw in the lower abdomen; straighten the left leg and move the centre of gravity to the bent right leg. Simultaneously, the left palm changes into a closed palm and swings, palm facing down, to the left side at shoulder height. Meanwhile, the right arm extends out to the right side with the closed palm facing down at shoulder height. Look straight ahead. (Fig. P.18)

Fig. P.18

8. EXHALING

Relax the anus, relax the pelvis and relax the lower abdomen; move the left foot to the side of the right foot and slowly straighten both legs. At the same time, lower both arms to the sides of the body as in the starting position. Look straight ahead.

Part 2

Repeat on right side, reversing all left/right directions.

Main points

1. The purpose of this exercise is to enhance the Lung functions so as to maintain the equilibrium of the Liver functions (in the Five Element theory this is called Metal controls Wood).

2. The mental focus during this exercise is on the acupoints Shangyang LI-1.

3. When making the eight character palm stretch the thumb and index finger as far apart as possible.

Standing Stress Prevention Exercise 5: Flower Displays Buddha

Starting position: Stand with the feet together, weight evenly distributed, body upright and relaxed with the hands hanging down at the sides of the body. Look straight ahead. (Fig. P.1)

Part 1

1. INHALING

Raise the anus, tilt the pelvis and draw in the lower abdomen; move the centre of gravity to the right foot, bend the right leg slightly and raise the left heel while rotating the arms inward until the palms rest on the front of the thighs. (Fig. P.19)

Fig. P.19

Without pause, turn the body 45 degrees to the left, step out with the left foot, Daoyin Diagonal Stepping, to the left diagonal and set the heel on the ground in a toe-up empty stance. Simultaneously, lightly brush the body with the palms vertically upwards until the acupoints Laogong PC-8 are covering acupoints Qimen LR-14. Look straight ahead. (Fig. P.20)

Fig. P.20

2. EXHALING

Relax the anus, relax the pelvis and relax the lower abdomen; slowly transfer the centre of gravity to the left foot and straighten the right leg in a left bow stance position. At the same time, lower the elbows and bring the palms close together with the fingers pointing upward.

Fig. P.21

Fig. P.22

Fig. P.23

Without pausing, turn the body slightly to the left (Fig. P.21) while raising the hands above the head, then hyperextend the hands so that the palms face upward and spread the fingers. Look up to the hands. (Fig. P.22)

3. INHALING

Raise the anus, tilt the pelvis and draw in the lower abdomen; straighten the left leg and transfer the centre of gravity to the bent right leg in a left toe-up empty stance and when the weight is fully on the right leg turn the body to face the front. Simultaneously, close up the fingers, bring the palms close together again, then change the palms into shang fists and lower the arms, brushing the sides of the body with the forearms until the hands are at the sides of the waist palm up. Look straight ahead. (Fig. P.23)

4. EXHALING

Relax the anus, relax the pelvis and relax the lower abdomen; slowly transfer the centre of gravity to the left foot and straighten the right leg in a left bow stance position. At the same time, lower the elbows, open the shang fists and bring the palms close together with the fingers pointing upward. Without pausing, turn the body slightly to the left while raising the hands above the head, then hyperextend the hands so that the palms face upward and spread the fingers. Look up to the hands.

5. INHALING

Raise the anus, tilt the pelvis and draw in the lower abdomen; straighten the left leg and transfer the centre of gravity to the bent right leg in a left toe-up empty stance and when the weight is fully on the right leg turn the body to face the front. Simultaneously, close up the fingers, bring the palms close together again, then change the palms into shang fists and lower the arms, brushing the sides of the body with the forearms until the hands are at the sides of the waist palm up. Look straight ahead. This is a repeat of step 3.

6. EXHALING

Relax the anus, relax the pelvis and relax the lower abdomen; slowly transfer the centre of gravity to the left foot and straighten the right leg in a left bow stance position. At the same time, lower the elbows, open the shang fists and bring the palms close together with the fingers pointing upward. Without pausing, turn the body slightly to the left while raising the hands above the head, then hyperextend the hands so that the palms face upward and spread the fingers. Look up to the hands. This is a repeat of step 4.

7. INHALING

Raise the anus, tilt the pelvis and draw in the lower abdomen; straighten the left leg and transfer the centre of gravity to the bent right leg in a left toe-up empty stance and when the weight is fully on the right leg turn the body to face the front. Simultaneously, close up the fingers, bring the palms close together again, then change the palms into shang fists and lower the arms, brushing the sides of the body with the forearms until the hands are at the sides of the waist palm up. Look straight ahead. This is a repeat of step 3.

Fig. P.24

8. EXHALING

Relax the anus, relax the pelvis and relax the lower abdomen; turn the shang fists into closed palms and rotate the arms inward until the palms face the rear. Swing the arms backward, upward and forward until they are at shoulder height, palm down, in front of the body. (Fig. P.24) Move the left foot to the side of the right foot, then slowly straighten the legs while lowering the arms to the sides of the body as in the starting position. Look straight ahead.

Part 2

Repeat on right side, reversing all left/right directions.

Main points

1. The purpose of this exercise is to enhance the Liver functions so as to maintain the equilibrium of the Spleen functions (in the Five Element theory this is called Wood controls Earth).

2. The mental focus during this exercise is on the acupoints Hegu LI-4.

3. Open eyes wide as fingers are spread during steps 2, 4 and 6.

Standing Stress Prevention Exercise 6: One Hand Supports Heaven

Starting position: Stand with the feet together, weight evenly distributed, body upright and relaxed with the hands hanging down at the sides of the body. Look straight ahead. (Fig. P.1)

Part 1

1. INHALING

Raise the anus, tilt the pelvis and draw in the lower abdomen; move the centre of gravity to the right foot, bend the right leg slightly and raise the left heel while rotating the arms outward and bringing the closed palms, fingertips pointing towards each other, palm up, in front of the lower abdomen. (Fig. P.25)

Fig. P.25

Without pause, take a step with the left foot to the left, Daoyin Side Stepping, so that the feet are approximately twice the width of the shoulders apart, move the centre of gravity to a position between both feet and then slowly straighten the legs. Simultaneously, raise the upturned palms in front of the body until they reach shoulder height. Look straight ahead. (Fig. P.26)

Fig. P.26

Fig. P.27

2. EXHALING

Relax the anus, relax the pelvis and relax the lower abdomen; without moving the feet slowly half squat on the heels into a horse stance. At the same time, turn the palms over and raise the left palm straight up above the left shoulder while turning the arm to finish palm up higher than the head. At the same time, lower the right palm to press down on the right thigh. Lean slightly to the right and look up at the left hand. (Fig. P.27)

3. INHALING

Raise the anus, tilt the pelvis, draw in the lower abdomen and without moving the feet slowly straighten the legs. Simultaneously, rotate both arms outward and bring both palms to the upturned position in front of the body as at the end of step 1. Look straight ahead.

4. EXHALING

Relax the anus, relax the pelvis and relax the lower abdomen; move the left foot to the side of the right foot and slowly straighten both legs. At the same time, turn the palms face down and lower them down the front and then to the sides of the body. Look straight ahead.

5. INHALING

Raise the anus, tilt the pelvis and draw in the lower abdomen; move the centre of gravity to the left foot, bend the left leg slightly and raise the right heel while rotating the arms outward and bringing the closed palms, fingertips pointing towards each other, palm up, in front of the lower abdomen.

Without pause, take a step with the right foot to the right, Daoyin Side Stepping, so that the feet are approximately twice the width of the shoulders apart, move the centre of gravity to a position between both feet and then slowly straighten the legs. Simultaneously, raise the upturned palms in front of the body until they reach shoulder height. Look straight ahead. This is the same as step 1 but in the opposite direction.

6. EXHALING

Relax the anus, relax the pelvis and relax the lower abdomen; without moving the feet slowly half squat on the heels into a horse stance. At the same time, turn the palms over and raise the right palm straight up above the right shoulder while turning the arm to finish palm up higher than the head. At the same time, lower the left palm to press down on the left thigh. Lean slightly to the left and look up at the right hand. This is the same as step 2 but in the opposite direction.

7. INHALING

Raise the anus, tilt the pelvis, draw in the lower abdomen and without moving the feet slowly straighten the legs. Simultaneously, rotate both arms outward and bring both palms to the upturned position in front of the body as at the end of step 1. Look straight ahead. This is the same as step 3 but in the opposite direction.

8. EXHALING

Relax the anus, relax the pelvis and relax the lower abdomen; move the right foot to the side of the left foot and slowly straighten both legs. At the same time, turn the palms face down and lower them down the front and then to the sides of the body. Look straight ahead.

Part 2

This is a repeat of Part 1.

Main points

1. The purpose of this exercise is to enhance the Spleen functions so as to maintain the equilibrium of the Kidney functions (in the Five Element theory this is called Earth controls Water).

2. The mental focus during this exercise is on the Lower Dantian.

3. After the arm is raised there is a brief pause while we feel the stretch before starting the exhale.

Standing Stress Prevention Exercise 7: Tapping Rendu

Starting position: Stand with the feet together, weight evenly distributed, body upright and relaxed with the hands hanging down at the sides of the body. Look straight ahead. (Fig. P.1)

Fig. P.28

Fig. P.29

Fig. P.30

Part 1

1. INHALING/EXHALING

Move the centre of gravity to the right foot, bend the right leg slightly and raise the left heel while changing the palms into hollow fists.

Without pause, take a step with the left foot to the left, Daoyin Side Stepping, so that the feet are a little more than shoulder-width apart; move the centre of gravity to a position between both feet and then slowly straighten the legs. Simultaneously, turn the body to the left and let the arms swing out and then tap with the eye of the hollow fists – right fist on Jiuwei RN-15 and left fist on Mingmen DU-4. Look to the left. (Fig. P.28, P.29, P.30)

2. INHALING/EXHALING

Turn to the right and let the arms swing out and then tap with the eye of the hollow fists – left fist on Jiuwei RN-15 and right fist on Mingmen DU-4. Look to the right.

3. INHALING/EXHALING

Turn to the left and let the arms swing out and then tap with the eye of the hollow fists – right fist on Jiuwei RN-15 and left fist on Mingmen DU-4. Look to the left.

4. INHALING/EXHALING

Turn to the right and let the arms swing out and then tap with the eye of the hollow fists – left fist on Jiuwei RN-15 and right fist on Mingmen DU-4. Look to the right. This is a repeat of step 2.

5. INHALING/EXHALING

Turn to the left and let the arms swing out and then tap with the eye of the hollow fists – right fist on Jiuwei RN-15 and left fist on Mingmen DU-4. Look to the left. This is a repeat of step 3.

6. INHALING/EXHALING

Turn to the right and let the arms swing out and then tap with the eye of the hollow fists – left fist on Jiuwei RN-15 and right fist on Mingmen DU-4. Look to the right. This is a repeat of step 2.

7. INHALING/EXHALING

Turn to the left and let the arms swing out and then tap with the eye of the hollow fists – right fist on Jiuwei RN-15 and left fist on Mingmen DU-4. Look to the left. This is a repeat of step 3.

8. INHALING/EXHALING

Turn to the right and let the arms swing out and then tap with the eye of the hollow fists – left fist on Jiuwei RN-15 and right fist on Mingmen DU-4. Look to the right. This is a repeat of step 2.

Part 2

The feet do not move and the tapping continues until step 8.

8. INHALING/EXHALING

No tapping. Bring feet together and place arms in starting position.

Main points

1. The purpose of this exercise is to connect and balance the energy system.

2. The mental focus during this exercise is on the acupoints being tapped, namely, Mingmen DU-4 and Jiuwei RN-15.

3. Part 2 begins with no movement of the feet, just a continuation of the turning and tapping.

4. The breathing in this exercise is more rapid as each count requires an inhale and an exhale and the tap is performed on the exhale. Inhale requires raising the anus, tilting the pelvis and drawing in the lower abdomen while exhale requires relaxing the anus, relaxing the pelvis and relaxing the lower abdomen.

Standing Stress Prevention Exercise 8: Sink Qi to Dantian

See the Standing Stress Relief routine for details of this exercise as it is exactly the same (pp.80–87).

SEATED STRESS PREVENTION ROUTINE

Stress Prevention Exercise 1: Taiji Breathing

See the Seated Stress Relief routine for details of this exercise as it is exactly the same (pp.88–93).

Seated Stress Prevention Exercise 2: Round Fan Covers the Moon

Starting position: Sit on the edge of the seat with the feet together, body upright and relaxed, hands placed on the upper thighs with fingers pointing to the knees. Look straight ahead. (Fig. PS.1)

Fig. PS.1

Part 1

1. INHALING

Raise the anus, tilt the pelvis and draw in the lower abdomen; raise the left heel while rotating the arms inward and bringing them in front of the body until the backs of the hands touch each other. Without pause, raise the hands up the centreline of the body to chest height, rolling them until the fingernails are pressed against each other. Then, flick the fingers apart, separate the hands to each side of the body while stepping with the left foot out to the side, Daoyin Side Stepping, until the left foot is in line with the left shoulder then place the heel down. Look at the left hand. (Fig. PS.2, PS.3)

Fig. PS.2   Fig. PS.3

2. EXHALING

Relax the anus, relax the pelvis and relax the lower abdomen; raise the left leg and cross it over the right thigh with the left knee close to the right knee, Daoyin Cross-over Stepping. Change the closed palms into open palms and swing the arms up in a leftward arc, hands close to each other, above the head and twist the body to face the left. Look up between the hands. (Fig. PS.4)

Fig. PS.4

3. INHALING

Raise the anus, tilt the pelvis and draw in the lower abdomen; close the palms and lower the arms to shoulder height still at the left side, then swing the arms horizontally to the front and place the left foot back on the ground. Look to the front beyond the hands. (Fig. PS.5, PS.6)

Fig. PS.5   Fig. PS.6

4. EXHALING

Relax the anus, relax the pelvis and relax the lower abdomen; bring the left foot to the side of the right foot while sinking the elbows. Then, slowly lower the hands to the thighs back to the starting position.

5. INHALING

Raise the anus, tilt the pelvis and draw in the lower abdomen; raise the right heel while rotating the arms inward and bringing them in front of the body until the backs of the hands touch each other. Without pause, raise the hands up the centreline of the body to chest height, rolling them until the fingernails are pressed against each other. Then, flick the fingers apart, separate the hands to each side of the body while stepping with the right foot out to the side, Daoyin Side Stepping, until the right foot is in line with the right shoulder then place the heel down. Look at the right hand. This is the same as step 1 with all left/right directions reversed.

6. EXHALING

Relax the anus, relax the pelvis and relax the lower abdomen; raise the right leg and cross it over the left thigh with the right knee close to the left knee, Daoyin Cross-over Stepping. Change the closed palm into an open palm and swing the arms up in a rightward arc above the head and twist the body to face the right. Look up between the hands. This is the same as step 2 with all left/right directions reversed.

7. INHALING

Raise the anus, tilt the pelvis and draw in the lower abdomen; close the palms and lower the arms to shoulder height still at the right side, then swing the arms horizontally to the front and place the right foot back on the ground. Look to the front beyond the hands. This is the same as step 3 with all left/right directions reversed.

8. EXHALING

Relax the anus, relax the pelvis and relax the lower abdomen; bring the right foot to the side of the left foot while sinking the elbows. Then, slowly lower the hands to the thighs back to the starting position. This is the same as step 4 with all left/right directions reversed.

Part 2

Repeat.

Main points

1. The purpose of this exercise is to enhance the Kidney functions so as to maintain the equilibrium of the Heart functions (in the Five Element theory this is called Water controls Fire).

2. The mental focus during this exercise is on the acupoint Mingmen DU-4.

3. When flicking the fingers apart they should make an audible sound.

4. Turn the waist fully when twisting the body to the side.

Seated Stress Prevention Exercise 3: Buffalo Ploughs the Land

Starting position: Sit on the edge of the seat with the feet together, body upright and relaxed, hands placed on the upper thighs with fingers pointing to the knees. Look straight ahead. (Fig. PS.1)

Part 1

1. INHALING

Raise the anus, tilt the pelvis and draw in the lower abdomen; raise the left heel while rotating the arms outward until the palms face forward. (Fig. PS.7)

Fig. PS.7

Without pause turn the body 45 degrees to the left, step out with the left foot, Daoyin Diagonal Stepping, to the left diagonal and set the heel on the ground in a toe-up empty stance. Then slowly lower the left foot to the ground and place weight on the ball of the left foot. Simultaneously, both arms sweep, palm up, vertically upward in front of the body to shoulder height. Look straight ahead beyond the hands. (Fig. PS.8)

Fig. PS.8

2. EXHALING

Relax the anus, relax the pelvis and relax the lower abdomen; pull the left foot and toes back into a toe-up empty stance. At the same time, turn the fingers inward until the fingertips point to the chest and then draw the hands to the chest while rotating both arms inward. When the backs of the hands face each other, with the fingertips pointing down, turn the body to face the front and lower the arms, lightly brushing the body with the tigermouth area of the dragon palm until the hands rest on the centreline of the thighs. Look straight ahead. (Fig. PS.9, PS.10)

Fig. PS.9   Fig. PS.10

3. INHALING

Raise the anus, tilt the pelvis and draw in the lower abdomen; turn the body 45 degrees to the left, then slowly lower the left foot to the ground and place weight on the ball of the left foot. Simultaneously, rotate the arms outward, palms facing forward, then sweep them upward in front of the body to shoulder height. Look straight ahead beyond the hands.

4. EXHALING

Relax the anus, relax the pelvis and relax the lower abdomen; pull the left foot and toes back into a toe-up empty stance. At the same time, turn the fingers inward until the fingertips point to the chest and then draw the hands to the chest while rotating both arms inward. When the backs of the hands face each other, with the fingertips pointing down, turn the body to face the front and lower the arms, lightly brushing the body with the tigermouth area of the dragon palm until the hands rest on the centreline of the thighs. Look straight ahead. This is a repeat of step 2.

5. INHALING

Raise the anus, tilt the pelvis and draw in the lower abdomen; turn the body 45 degrees to the left, then slowly lower the left foot to the ground and place weight on the ball of the left foot. Simultaneously, rotate the arms outward, palms facing forward, then sweep them upward in front of the body to shoulder height. Look straight ahead beyond the hands. This is a repeat of step 3.

6. EXHALING

Relax the anus, relax the pelvis and relax the lower abdomen; pull the left foot and toes back into a toe-up empty stance. At the same time, turn the fingers inward until the fingertips point to the chest and then draw the hands to the chest while rotating both arms inward. When the backs of the hands face each other, with the fingertips pointing down, turn the body to face the front and lower the arms, lightly brushing the body with the tigermouth area of the dragon palm until the hands rest on the centreline of the thighs. Look straight ahead. This is a repeat of step 2.

7. INHALING

Raise the anus, tilt the pelvis and draw in the lower abdomen; turn the body 45 degrees to the left, then slowly lower the left foot to the ground and place weight on the ball of the left foot. Simultaneously, rotate the arms outward, palms facing forward, then sweep them upward in front of the body to shoulder height. Look straight ahead beyond the hands. This is a repeat of step 3.

8. EXHALING

Relax the anus, relax the pelvis and relax the lower abdomen; pull the left foot and toes back into a toe-up empty stance. At the same time, turn the fingers inward until the fingertips point to the chest and then draw the hands to the chest while rotating both arms inward. When the backs of the hands face each other, with the fingertips pointing down, turn the body to face the front, bring the left foot back to the side of the right foot and lower the arms, lightly brushing the body with the tigermouth area of the dragon palm until the hands rest on the centreline of the thighs. Finally, rotate the arms outward until the palms are now in the original starting position. Look straight ahead.

Part 2

Repeat, reversing all left/right directions.

Main points

1. The purpose of this exercise is to enhance the Heart functions so as to maintain the equilibrium of the Lung functions (in the Five Element theory this is called Fire controls Metal).

2. The mental focus during this exercise is on the acupoints Laogong PC-8.

3. When raising the arms to the front, rotate the arms outward and to raise the little finger edge of the palm the higest.

Seated Stress Prevention Exercise 4: Distinguished Lord Combs Hair

Starting position: Sit on the edge of the seat with the feet together, body upright and relaxed, hands placed on the upper thighs with fingers pointing to the knees. Look straight ahead. (Fig. PS.1)

Part 1

1. INHALING

Raise the anus, tilt the pelvis and draw in the lower abdomen; raise the left heel and slightly separate the legs, Daoyin Side Stepping, until the left foot is in line with the left shoulder then place the heel down while swinging the left arm out to the side with the palm facing the rear. Then repeat the actions with the right leg and right arm. (Fig PS.11)

Fig. PS.11

Without pause, push both arms backward and upward while turning the body slightly to the left. When the arms reach shoulder height, rotate the arms outward until the palms face forward.

Continuing, the left arm now bends and the left closed palm is placed on the back of the head. At the same time, the right arm swings leftward across the body and the right closed palm is placed against the left jaw line. Look to the left side. (Fig. PS.12)

Fig. PS.12

2. EXHALING

Relax the anus, relax the pelvis and relax the lower abdomen; press both feet lightly to the ground, turn the body to face forward and draw the right elbow to the rear, sweeping the right closed palm off the face and stopping when the palm is face up at the right side of the ribs. Meanwhile, the left elbow swings to the front allowing the left palm to brush the hair, then the arm extends forward in front of the body at shoulder height with the left closed palm changing into an eight character palm. Look at the eight character palm. (Fig. PS.13)

Fig. PS.13

3. INHALING

Raise the anus, tilt the pelvis and draw in the lower abdomen; turn the body slightly to the right, change the left eight character palm into a closed palm and sweep it rightward across the body and place it against the right jaw line. Meanwhile, the right closed palm moves in a circular sweep, downward, backward and upward and is placed on the back of the head. Look to the right side.

4. EXHALING

Relax the anus, relax the pelvis and relax the lower abdomen; press both feet lightly to the ground, turn the body to face forward and draw the left elbow to the rear, sweeping the left closed palm off the face and stopping when the palm is face up at the left side of the ribs. Meanwhile, the right elbow swings to the front allowing the right palm to brush the hair, then the arm extends forward in front of the body at shoulder height with the right closed palm changing into an eight character palm. Look at the eight character palm.

5. INHALING

Raise the anus, tilt the pelvis and draw in the lower abdomen; turn the body slightly to the left, change the right eight character palm into a closed palm and sweep it leftward across the body and place it against the left jaw line. Meanwhile, the left closed palm moves in a circular sweep, downward, backward and upward and is placed on the back of the head. Look to the left side.

6. EXHALING

Relax the anus, relax the pelvis and relax the lower abdomen; press both feet lightly to the ground, turn the body to face forward and draw the right elbow to the rear, sweeping the right closed palm off the face and stopping when the palm is face up at the right side of the ribs. Meanwhile, the left elbow swings to the front allowing the left palm to brush the hair, then the arm extends forward in front of the body at shoulder height with the left closed palm changing into an eight character palm. Look at the eight character palm. This is a repeat of step 2.

7. INHALING

Raise the anus, tilt the pelvis and draw in the lower abdomen; the left palm changes into a closed palm and swings, palm facing down, to the left side at shoulder height. Meanwhile, the right arm extends out to the right side with the closed palm facing down at shoulder height. Look straight ahead. (Fig. PS.14)

Fig. PS.14

8. EXHALING

Relax the anus, relax the pelvis and relax the lower abdomen; raise the heels and bring the right foot inwards and then place the left next to it. At the same time, sweep both arms down and place the hands on the thighs back in the starting position. Look straight ahead.

Part 2

Repeat, reversing all left/right directions.

Main points

1. The purpose of this exercise is to enhance the Lung functions so as to maintain the equilibrium of the Liver functions (in the Five Element theory this is called Metal controls Wood).

2. The mental focus during this exercise is on the acupoints Shangyang LI-1.

3. When making the eight character palm stretch the thumb and index finger as far apart as possible.

Seated Stress Prevention Exercise 5: Flower Displays Buddha

Starting position: Sit on the edge of the seat with the feet together, body upright and relaxed, hands placed on the upper thighs with fingers pointing to the knees. Look straight ahead. (Fig. PS.1)

Part 1

1. INHALING

Raise the anus, tilt the pelvis and draw in the lower abdomen; raise the left heel but do not move the hands.

Without pause turn the body 45 degrees to the left, step out with the left foot, Daoyin Diagonal Stepping, to the left diagonal and set the heel on the ground in a toe-up empty stance. Simultaneously, lightly brush the body with the palms vertically upwards until the acupoints Laogong PC-8 are covering acupoints Qimen LR-14. Look straight ahead to the left diagonal. (Fig. PS.15, PS.16)

Fig. PS.15   Fig. PS.16

2. EXHALING

Relax the anus, relax the pelvis and relax the lower abdomen; lower the left foot to the ground and apply some pressure to put weight onto the ball of the foot. At the same time, lower the elbows and bring the palms close together with the fingers pointing upward. Without pausing, turn the body slightly to the left while raising the hands above the head, then hyperextend the hands so that the palms face upward and spread the fingers. Look up to the hands. (Fig. PS.17)

Fig. PS.17

3. INHALING

Raise the anus, tilt the pelvis and draw in the lower abdomen; pull the left foot and toes back into a toe-up empty stance and turn the body to face the front. Simultaneously, close up the fingers, bring the palms close together again, then change the palms into shang fists and lower the arms, brushing the sides of the body with the forearms until the hands are at the sides of the waist palm up. Look straight ahead. (Fig. PS.18)

Fig. PS.18

4. EXHALING

Relax the anus, relax the pelvis and relax the lower abdomen; lower the left foot to the ground and apply some pressure to put weight onto the ball of the foot. At the same time, lower the elbows, open the shang fists and bring the palms close together with the fingers pointing upward. Without pausing, turn the body slightly to the left while raising the hands above the head, then hyperextend the hands so that the palms face upward and spread the fingers. Look up to the hands.

5. INHALING

Raise the anus, tilt the pelvis and draw in the lower abdomen; pull the left foot and toes back into a toe-up empty stance and turn the body to face the front. Simultaneously, close up the fingers, bring the palms close together again, then change the palms into shang fists and lower the arms, brushing the sides of the body with the forearms until the hands are at the sides of the waist palm up. Look straight ahead. This is a repeat of step 3.

6. EXHALING

Relax the anus, relax the pelvis and relax the lower abdomen; lower the left foot to the ground and apply some pressure to put weight onto the ball of the foot. At the same time, lower the elbows, open the shang fists and bring the palms close together with the fingers pointing upward. Without pausing, turn the body slightly to the left while raising the hands above the head, then hyperextend the hands so that the palms face upward and spread the fingers. Look up to the hands. This is a repeat of step 4.

7. INHALING

Raise the anus, tilt the pelvis and draw in the lower abdomen; pull the left foot and toes back into a toe-up empty stance and turn the body to face the front. Simultaneously, close up the fingers, bring the palms close together again, then change the palms into shang fists and lower the arms, brushing the sides of the body with the forearms until the hands are at the sides of the waist palm up. Look straight ahead. This is a repeat of step 3.

8. EXHALING

Relax the anus, relax the pelvis and relax the lower abdomen; turn the shang fists into closed palms and rotate the arms inward until the palms face the rear. Swing the arms backward, upward and forward until they are at shoulder height, palm down, in front of the body. Move the left foot to the side of the right foot, then slowly lower the hands to the thighs back to the starting position. Look straight ahead.

Part 2

Repeat, reversing all left/right directions.

Main points

1. The purpose of this exercise is to enhance the Liver functions so as to maintain the equilibrium of the Spleen functions (in the Five Element theory this is called Wood controls Earth).

2. The mental focus during this exercise is on the acupoints Hegu LI-4.

3. Open eyes wide as fingers are spread during steps 2, 4 and 6.

Seated Stress Prevention Exercise 6: One Hand Supports Heaven

Starting position: Sit on the edge of the seat with the feet together, body upright and relaxed, hands placed on the upper thighs with fingers pointing to the knees. Look straight ahead. (Fig. PS.1)

Part 1

1. INHALING

Raise the anus, tilt the pelvis and draw in the lower abdomen; raise the left heel and slightly separate the legs, Daoyin Side Stepping, until the left foot is in line with the left shoulder then place the heel down while turning the left palm face upward. Then repeat the actions with the right leg and right arm and finish with the fingertips pointing to each other. Without pause raise the hands straight up until they are at shoulder level. Look straight ahead. (Fig. PS.19, PS.20)

Fig. PS.19   Fig. PS.20

2. EXHALING

Relax the anus, relax the pelvis and relax the lower abdomen; apply some slight pressure to the ground to put weight onto the heels while turning the palms over and raising the left palm straight up above the left shoulder, turning the arm to finish palm up, higher than the head. At the same time, lower the right palm to press down on the right thigh. Lean slightly to the right and look up at the left hand. (Fig. PS.21)

Fig. PS.21

3. INHALING

Raise the anus, tilt the pelvis, draw in the lower abdomen; change the direction of the pressure on the ground to move the weight to the balls of the feet, rotate both arms outward and bring both palms to the upturned position in front of the body as at the end of step one. Look straight ahead.

4. EXHALING

Relax the anus, relax the pelvis and relax the lower abdomen; apply some slight pressure to the ground to put weight onto the heels. At the same time, turn the palms face down and lower them down to the thighs, back in the starting position. Look straight ahead.

5. INHALING

Raise the anus, tilt the pelvis and draw in the lower abdomen; change the direction of the pressure on the ground to move the weight to the balls of the feet, turn the palms face upward with the fingertips pointing to each other and, without pause, raise the hands straight up until they are at shoulder level. Look straight ahead.

6. EXHALING

Relax the anus, relax the pelvis and relax the lower abdomen; apply some slight pressure to the ground to put weight onto the heels while turning the palms over and raising the right palm straight up above the right shoulder, turning the arm to finish palm up, higher than the head. At the same time, lower the left palm to press down on the left thigh. Lean slightly to the left and look up at the right hand.

7. INHALING

Raise the anus, tilt the pelvis, draw in the lower abdomen; change the direction of the pressure on the ground to move the weight to the balls of the feet, rotate both arms outward and bring both palms to the upturned position in front of the body as at the end of step one. Look straight ahead.

8. EXHALING

Relax the anus, relax the pelvis and relax the lower abdomen; raise the heels and bring the right foot inwards and then place the left next to it. At the same time, turn the palms face down and lower them down to the thighs, back to the starting position. Look straight ahead.

Part 2

Repeat, reversing all left/right directions.

Main points

1. The purpose of this exercise is to enhance the Spleen functions so as to maintain the equilibrium of the Kidney functions (in the Five Element theory this is called Earth controls Water).

2. The mental focus during this exercise is on the Lower Dantian.

3. After the arm is raised there is a brief pause while we feel the stretch before starting the exhale.

Seated Stress Prevention Exercise 7: Tapping Rendu

Starting position: Sit on the edge of the seat with the feet together, body upright and relaxed, hands placed on the upper thighs with fingers pointing to the knees. Look straight ahead. (Fig. PS.1)

Part 1

1. INHALING/EXHALING

Raise the left heel and slightly separate the legs, Daoyin Side Stepping, until the left foot is in line with the left shoulder then place the heel down while changing the left palm to a hollow fist. Then repeat the actions with the right leg and right hand. (Fig. PS.22)

Fig. PS.22

Without pause, turn the body to the left and let the arms swing out and then tap with the eye of the hollow fists – right fist on Jiuwei RN-15 and left fist on Mingmen DU-4. Look to the left. (Fig. PS.23)

2. INHALING/EXHALING

Turn to the right and let the arms swing out and then tap with the eye of the hollow fists – left fist on Jiuwei RN-15 and right fist on Mingmen DU-4. Look to the right. (Fig. PS.24)

Fig. PS.23   Fig. PS.24

3. INHALING/EXHALING

Turn to the left and let the arms swing out and then tap with the eye of the hollow fists – right fist on Jiuwei RN-15 and left fist on Mingmen DU-4. Look to the left.

4. INHALING/EXHALING

Turn to the right and let the arms swing out and then tap with the eye of the hollow fists – left fist on Jiuwei RN-15 and right fist on Mingmen DU-4. Look to the right. This is a repeat of step 2.

5. INHALING/EXHALING

Turn to the left and let the arms swing out and then tap with the eye of the hollow fists – right fist on Jiuwei RN-15 and left fist on Mingmen DU-4. Look to the left. This is a repeat of step 3.

6. INHALING/EXHALING

Turn to the right and let the arms swing out and then tap with the eye of the hollow fists – left fist on Jiuwei RN-15 and right fist on Mingmen DU-4. Look to the right. This is a repeat of step 2.

7. INHALING/EXHALING

Turn to the left and let the arms swing out and then tap with the eye of the hollow fists – right fist on Jiuwei RN-15 and left fist on Mingmen DU-4. Look to the left. This is a repeat of step 3.

8. INHALING/EXHALING

Turn to the right and let the arms swing out and then tap with the eye of the hollow fists – left fist on Jiuwei RN-15 and right fist on Mingmen DU-4. Look to the right. This is a repeat of step 2.

Part 2

Continue the tapping until step 8.

8. INHALING/EXHALING.

No tapping. Raise the heels and bring the right foot inwards and then place the left next to it. At the same time, sweep both arms down and place the hands on the thighs back in the starting position. Look straight ahead.

Main points

1. The purpose of this exercise is to connect and balance the energy system.

2. The mental focus during this exercise is on the acupoints being tapped, namely, Mingmen DU-4 and Jiuwei RN-15.

3. Part 2 begins with no movement of the feet, just a continuation of the turning and tapping.

4. The breathing in this exercise is more rapid as each count requires an inhale and an exhale and the tap is performed on the exhale. Inhale requires raising the anus, tilting the pelvis and drawing in the lower abdomen while exhale requires relaxing the anus, relaxing the pelvis and relaxing the lower abdomen.

Seated Stress Prevention Exercise 8: Sink Qi to Dantian

See the Seated Stress Relief routine for details of this exercise as it is exactly the same (pp.121–127).

Principles of
Action

General Principles of Action

Every individual exercise in these stress routines has a purpose and a mechanism of action which fulfils that purpose. However, the mechanisms behind individual Qigong exercises can be quite complex. This section, therefore, presents a simplified description of the fundamental processes involved, "Qigong Principles of Action 101," as it were, along with an explanation of what is required for an exercise to qualify as Qigong.

According to the *Huang Di Nei Jing Ling Shu* (*The Yellow Emperor's Internal Classic: Spiritual Pivot*), an ancient Chinese medical text, the internal organs have 12 source points. These points are located at or near to the wrists and ankles, known as the "four gates," and manipulating them has a direct effect on their associated internal organs. Thus, the four gates can exert control over the health of the internal organs.

This is of great significance for all Daoyin types of Qigong that tend to exploit physical movements, especially those known as Anqiao movements. The Chinese word *qiao* has a general meaning of "to lift up." When prefaced by the word *an*, "to press," it gives a more specific meaning in Daoyin terms. *Anqiao* then refers to a kind of self-administered acupressure which results from the raising and lowering of the hands and feet by flexing the wrists and ankles and this, in turn, exerts an influence over the internal organs.

Anqiao movements are commonly referred to as the opening and closing of the source points and if we view Qi flow in terms of fluid dynamics we can make an analogy with Bernoulli's Principle (named after Dutch–Swiss mathematician Daniel Bernoulli) to give us an understanding of what is happening during these actions.

Bernoulli's Principle states that as the speed of a moving fluid increases, the pressure within the fluid decreases.

In practice this means that as we move the acupoint towards the closed position we are narrowing the channel which increases the velocity of the Qi flow and decreases its pressure. When it is fully closed the Qi volume and pressure increases upstream of the dam. Movement towards the fully opened channel reduces the velocity of Qi flow but increases its pressure. Examples are the jet exhaust (opening acupoints) and the firehose nozzle (closing acupoints).

This gives us a certain amount of control over the flow of energy through the physical movement of the body.

It should also be noted that the results of Daoyin Anqiao can be modified by the specific mechanisms of particular movements.

One very important distinction between Qigong of the Daoyin type and other types of Qigong is that the Yang aspects of the Daoyin movements are performed with an effort. The Yin part of Daoyin is the relaxation after the Yang stretching movements. This is a point that is often overlooked.

Before detailing the mechanisms involved in each movement there needs to be some basic information about the general principles behind all Qigong.

The Three Regulations

The requirement that differentiates Qigong from other types of exercise is known as the "Three Regulations" (*san tiao*). This refers to the three methods employed simultaneously to improve an individual's health, which are the regulation of the body, the regulation of the breath and the regulation of the mind.

Clearly, the mechanism of action must be through the "Three Regulations." Movement of the body, control of the breathing and focus of mind are simultaneously adjusted to provide the appropriate action for the purpose of the individual exercise.

The success in Qigong training is directly related to the coordination and correctness of the "Three Regulations."

REGULATING THE BODY

The physical movements in the individual exercises make the body twist, turn and bend in set sequences, which:

- exert physical pressure on muscle, tendon, bones (tuina massage) and certain targeted acupoints (acupressure) to develop strength, flexibility and keep Qi and blood moving

- apply pressure to specific internal organs (fuzang or visceral massage) to remove Stagnation

- stretch and rotate the jingluo (energy channels throughout the body) to "dredge" the channels to remove blockages and keep the Qi flowing freely.

REGULATING THE BREATHING

Qigong primarily uses two types of abdominal breathing. The first, Normal Breathing (sometimes called Buddhist Breathing), involves the expansion of the lower abdomen during inhalation and contraction during exhalation. The second, Reverse Breathing (sometimes called Daoist Breathing), involves contraction of the lower abdomen during inhalation and expansion during exhalation. These two types of breathing are the Yin and Yang of each other and as such they are complementary. Normal Breathing is very efficient at gathering energy but less efficient at moving energy and is generally used at the beginning and end of Qigong routines, whereas Reverse Breathing is very efficient at moving energy but less efficient at gathering energy and is generally used throughout the active part of the routines.

Breathing is one of the most significant aspects of Qigong (which can also be translated as "breathing exercise"). The breathing is significant because it is the only one of the Three Regulations that can actually increase the levels of energy in the body. Regulating the mind and regulating the body both expend energy but correct breathing can increase energy. In terms of Yin and Yang, food and drink provide Yin energy and the air that we breathe provides Yang energy. To paraphrase a simple Chinese saying which highlights the relative importance of these sources of energy, "to see which source of energy is most important do not eat for ten minutes and then do not breathe for ten minutes and you quickly discover the most important source of energy."

In the Qigong presented here Normal Breathing is used at the beginning and end of each routine and Reverse Breathing during all the physical movements.

REGULATING THE MIND

Under normal circumstances the mind consumes a great deal of energy. When stress enters the equation the consumption increases excessively. Regulating the mind reduces this consumption and also concentrates the energy into the healing process. This is achieved through "stillness," a special state of inner quiet or quiescence.

This stillness of mind in Daoyin is different from our normal ideas of stillness as it refers to dynamic stillness (a Yang within the Yin) where the mental process is not dispersed in all directions but is focused with the intent.

Using light as an analogy, a light bulb diffuses light in all directions, the use of a reflector will focus the light in a particular direction and the use of a laser will concentrate light into a much more powerful coherent beam of light.

Under normal circumstances the mind is like the light bulb; mental activity is diffused in all directions. When we "focus" the mind by eliminating distracting thoughts we are using a reflector to strengthen the beam and give it direction and, finally, we concentrate the mind using "intent" to give a very powerful, coherent output.

Practice of regulating the mind moves us from diffusion to coherence until movement of mind coordinated with body and breath becomes a unified whole. When this occurs the Qi follows the intent and the blood follows the Qi and healing is the result.

TILTING THE PELVIS AND RAISING THE ANUS

Another general rule of Daoyin Yangsheng exercise is that with each inhalation (Yang breath), the pelvis is tilted upwards to the front and at the same time the anus is pulled upwards while, during exhalation (Yin breath), the abdomen and the anus have to relax.

One of the primary energy circuits in Qigong is the Xiaozhoutian (Small Heavenly Cycle), which is composed of the Dumai (Governor Vessel) and Renmai (Conception Vessel), and where these channels connect with each other is referred to as a "magpie bridge." Pulling up the anus while inhaling has a double action on Qi flow; in conjunction with Reverse Breathing it encourages Qi to move from the Lower Dantian reservoir and into the Xiaozhoutian, and at the same time it enhances the lower magpie bridge connection. Placing the tongue on the roof of the mouth connects the upper magpie bridge.

Tilting the pelvis upwards to the front while inhaling improves posture as it physically aligns the body's structure by straightening the lower spine. Improved posture allows the essential body fluids (blood, lymph, Qi and mind) to move smoothly – like water through an uncoiled hose pipe.

Each full breath, one inhale and one exhale, represents one energy pulsation. Just as the heart has to contract and then release in order to pump blood, so the body and breath have to combine to contract and release in order to pump Qi. The pelvic tilt and anal contraction are a part of this pumping action.

As a generalization, there are only four basic movements of Qi: up, down, in and out. Therefore, hands rising have a tendency to lead energy upward, hands lowering have a tendency to lead energy downward, hands moving outward have a tendency to lead energy to expand and hands moving inward have a tendency to lead energy to contract. However, specific exercises employ many different hand positions to produce many different specific results, through Anqiao and other principles. These specific results will be explained for the individual exercises.

By contrast there are only a few different types of stepping. The Stress routines employ three basic Daoyin Stepping actions: Side Stepping, Diagonal Stepping and Cross-over Stepping.

In Daoyin Side Stepping the heel is lifted leaving the big toe pointing to the ground and as the foot moves to the side the big toe remains pointing at the ground. This stimulates Dadun LR-1 and Yinbai SP-1 in the big toe promoting the flow of energy along the Liver and Spleen channels; it also stimulates Taichong LR-3, the Liver source point, and Taibai SP-3, the Spleen source point, which has a direct effect on the Liver and Spleen organs. So, Daoyin Side Stepping strengthens the Liver and Spleen and reinforces the internal energy of their channels.

In Daoyin Diagonal Stepping, as the foot is lifted and moved to the diagonal, it is done in the same manner and with the same result as in Side Stepping. The difference this time is that at the end of the diagonal movement the toes are pulled back and the heel placed on the ground, which is why it is also called Daoyin Toe-up Stepping. This stimulates Yongquan KI-1, promoting Qi flow through the Kidney channel and also stimulates Taixi KI-3, the Kidney source point, which directly affects the Kidneys themselves. Placing the heel down and pulling the toes back also stimulates the Yinqiaomai and Yangqiaomai – two of the "extra" channels which run through the heel and help to regulate the Yin and Yang balance in the body.

In the Daoyin Cross-over Stepping it is the forcing back of the toes on the rear foot that gives a very strong action on Yongquan KI-1 and Taixi Ki-3, Kidney source point, and the twist of the body that gives a powerful "wringing out" action to dredge the channel.

To summarize: Side Stepping has actions on the Liver and Spleen; Diagonal Stepping has actions on the Liver, Spleen, Kidneys and Yin/Yang regulation; and Cross-over Stepping has very strong actions on the Kidneys.

The Daoyin exercises have two phases, Yang and Yin. The Yang, or dynamic, phase is where the main part of the movement takes place, the twisting, turning and point pressing, etc., to activate the individual mechanisms for that exercise and the Yin, or passive, phase is equally as important because it is during this phase that everything actually happens. To use the simple analogy of throwing a ball, the Yang phase is the movement of the body and arm as the ball is swung forwards and the Yin phase is when the ball is released – it is only at that point that the ball goes anywhere. Throwing the ball is only successful because the Yang and Yin phases work together. The Yin phases of the Daoyin exercises are those movements that return the body to the starting position. They are as important for the success of the exercise and require as much mindfulness as the Yang phases.

Bearing this in mind, it should also be noted that, although each of the exercises has a designated mental focus point according to the purpose of that exercise, during the Yin phase, i.e. returning to the starting position, the mental focus will generally be on the Lower Dantian.

Specific Principles of Action

The exercises "Taiji Breathing" and "Sink Qi to Dantian" are common to both routines and so are described separately first.

Principles of Taiji Breathing

This exercise is the opening sequence and its purpose is to create a transition from the everyday ordinary body/breath/mind state to a tranquil/eased/focused state and to initiate the Three Regulations required throughout the remainder of the Qigong routine.

The first stage of this exercise begins with inhaling and the bodyweight moving over the balls of the feet as the hands are raised overhead. The reason for this is that as the weight reaches the balls of the feet it applies pressure to the Yongquan K-1 acupoints which encourages the flow of Qi from the Lower Dantian to the lower limbs. Meanwhile, the arms are slowly raised creating a physical expansion of the chest cavity which initiates deep, slow breathing.

While the arms are being raised the mind is concentrated on the Laogong PC-8 acupoints on the palms of the hands to guide the Qi from the Lower Dantian to the upper limbs. As the hands move over the head this also helps the Qi to reach the top of the head.

The Qi flow itself is aided by Reverse Breathing which pushes the Qi from the lower abdomen out into the Meridian system.

The result of stage 1 is a slow pulse of energy spreading out from the Lower Dantian centre to reach all the body extremities.

The second stage of this exercise involves exhaling and the bodyweight moving from the balls of the feet to the heels as the hands are lowered. The reason for this is that as the weight reaches the heels it removes the pressure from the Yongquan K-1 acupoints which encourages the return flow of Qi from the lower limbs to the Lower Dantian. Meanwhile, the arms are gradually lowered creating a physical collapse of the chest cavity which slowly forces the depleted air outward.

While the arms are being lowered the mental concentration is changed from Laogong PC-8 acupoint to the Lower Dantian to guide the Qi from the upper limbs back to the Lower Dantian. The downward movement of the hands also encourages the Qi to sink down from the head.

The Qi flow itself is aided by Reverse Breathing which gathers the Qi from the Meridian system and collects it in the lower abdomen.

The result of stage 2 is a slow pulse of energy returning from the extremities to the Lower Dantian centre.

Throughout the exercise all the acupuncture source points on the wrists and feet are being gently stimulated for the dual purpose of encouraging equilibrium in their appropriate internal organs and preparing those same organs for the stimulation to come during the subsequent exercises in the routine.

By repeating these powerful rhythmic movements we "relax and energize" the body, "soften and deepen" the breath, and "calm and focus" the mind, achieving the "Three Regulations."

Principles of Sink Qi to Dantian

This exercise is the closing sequence and its purpose is to return the body/breath/mind to their normal, but now improved, states.

The first half of this exercise is concerned with bringing any excess Qi that might have gathered in the Upper Dantian down to the Middle Dantian, a staging post on its way to the Lower Dantian.

This is achieved by inhaling and moving the bodyweight to the balls of the feet to apply pressure to the Yongquan K-1 acupoints which encourages Qi to flow downwards. At the same time the hands are raised, charged with Qi and placed on the forehead in preparation for drawing the energy down. During this inhalation phase the mind is focused on the Middle Dantian and it is this mental concentration coupled with physically raising the hands upward *away* from the body that blocks any more Qi from lodging in the Upper Dantian.

During the exhalation phase the bodyweight moves from the balls of the feet to the heels which removes the pressure from the Yongquan K-1 acupoints thus encouraging the return flow of Qi from the lower limbs to the Lower Dantian. Meanwhile, the hands brushing from the forehead to the back of the head and then down the neck to the front of the chest is coupled with the mental concentration guiding the Qi from the Upper Dantian down to the Middle Dantian.

The second half of this exercise is concerned with bringing any excess Qi that might have gathered in the Middle Dantian down to the Lower Dantian, our main energy centre.

This is achieved by continuing to move the bodyweight back and forth for exactly the reasons as in the first half. Now, however, when inhaling, the hands are raised, charged with Qi and placed together over the Middle Dantian. During this inhalation phase the mind is focused on the Lower Dantian and it is this mental concentration coupled with physically raising the hands upward *away* from the body that blocks any more Qi from lodging in the Middle Dantian.[1]

While exhaling, the chest physically sinks inward when the hands brush downward and these actions reinforce the descending

---

1 "Taiji Breathing," "Swirling Water" and "Swimming Fish Flaps Its Tail" can be combined with this exercise to form a mini-set for regulating and calming.

of Qi which is guided by the mental concentration moving from the Middle Dantian down to the Lower Dantian.

The overall result is a gathering of surplus energies into the Lower Dantian. With the mind being focused on the Lower Dantian as well this means that our energy, our mind and our centre are now coordinated in one place which leaves us in an enhanced and balanced state.

Stress Relief Principles of Action

Traditional Chinese Medicine recognizes three main inter-connected syndromes related to stress: Liver-Qi Stagnation (the most common), Disturbance of the Mind and Phlegm-Fire Disturbing Upwards.

Liver-Qi Stagnation can produce a host of symptoms associated with stress because one of the main tasks of the Liver is to ensure the smooth flow of energy throughout the body. If the Liver-Qi is stuck then it can create a problem anywhere in the body which, in turn, creates the different symptoms. When the Stagnation turns to Fire the problems, mental, physical and emotional, become exacerbated. Therefore, the therapeutic principle is to eliminate Fire from the Liver and remove Liver-Qi Stagnation.

At the simplest level the mind here refers not only to mental functions but also to an individual's spirit and emotional state. Therefore, the therapeutic principle of "Calming the Mind" has the meaning of bringing the mental functions, the emotions and the spirit back to a peaceful state.

Fire from the Heart and Liver mixed with Phlegm can lead to the common stress symptoms of emotional instability, insomnia, irritability and over thinking. Therefore, the therapeutic principle is to eliminate Fire from the Heart and Liver and to dispel Phlegm.

The following exercises are designed to deal with these three syndromes and are structured as follows.

The structure of the Stress Relief routine

The routine consists of eight exercises grouped into three sections.

Section 1	1. Taiji Breathing	Opening
	2. Swirling Water	To calm the mind
Section 2	3. Eagle Soaring in the Sky	To eliminate Fire from the Heart and Liver and to dispel Phlegm
	4. Black Dragon Displays Its Talons	To remove Liver-Qi Stagnation
	5. Dragon Hiding in the Blue Sea	To eliminate Fire from the Heart and Liver and to dispel Phlegm
	6. Swirling Clouds	To remove Liver-Qi Stagnation
Section 3	7. Swimming Fish Flaps Its Tail	To calm the mind
	8. Sink Qi to Dantian	Closing

The purpose of Section 1 is to prepare the body and mind for the Yang, active exercises to follow.

The purpose of Section 2 is to rid the body of Fire, Phlegm and Stagnation. Exercises 5 and 6 reinforce and extend the range of Exercises 3 and 4.

The purpose of Section 3 is to return the body and mind back to a Yin, peaceful state.

Exercises 1, "Taiji Breathing" and 8, "Sink Qi to Dantian" are common to the Stress Prevention routine as well and have already been described.

The principles of the relief Exercises 2 to 7 are described below. These exercises are designed to work with stage 2 of the chronic stress situation, the "fight or flight" or physical response.

Principle of Swirling Water

PURPOSE

This exercise deals with the "Disturbance of the Mind" syndrome.

This exercise has the same function as "Swimming Fish Flaps Its Tail" but Swirling Water is of a Yang nature compared to the Yin nature of the "Swimming Fish Flaps Its Tail." These movements lead to a more dynamic quiescence.

ACUPOINTS UTILIZED

The primary acupoints for "Calming the Mind" used in this exercise are: Yongquan KI-1, Taixi KI-3, Yinbai SP-1, Taichong LR-3 and Jiexi ST-41, activated by the footwork; Shenmen HT-7, Daling PC-7 and Xinshu BL-15, activated by movements of the arms and torso; and Laogong PC-8, activated by the mind.

ACTIONS DESCRIBED

Only the actions of the first six steps, the Yang or active phase, are described. Steps 7 and 8 belong to the Yin or passive phase which serves to return the body to the starting position. All other movements in the exercise are repeats.

DAOYIN FOOTWORK

The footwork used throughout this exercise is the Daoyin Diagonal Stepping and the weight-shift from bow stance to toe-up stance. This footwork serves several functions. It is used here particularly for its stimulation of Yinbai SP-1, Taichong LR-3, Yongquan KI-1, Taixi KI-3 and Jiexi ST-41, which together have a powerful calming effect on the mind. It also acts on Yinqiao mai and Yangqiao mai to regulate the Yin and Yang balance in the body.

DAOYIN BODYWORK

Step 1 involves inhaling with Reverse Breathing which moves the Qi out of the Lower Dantian; the hands rising up close in front of the chest keeps the thoracic cavity slightly depressed which prevents the Qi from moving into the chest and so it is guided to flow up the spine to Dazhui DU-14 just below the seventh cervical vertebrae, a point from which the Qi flow branches into the arms.

While exhaling during step 2 the arms push forward and the mental focus on Laogong PC-8 guides the Qi from Dazhui DU-14 down the arms and to the hands while at the same time the physical movement slowly closes the three source points at the wrist crease to increase the Qi pressure on Shenmen HT-7 and Daling PC-7.

The conclusion of step 2 involves tilting the palms slightly up to add a little extra pressure to the Heart and Pericardium points.

Step 3 pushes one arm to the rear and this action changes the closed source points (see pp.185–186) to open source points and applies pressure to Xinshu BL-15, maintaining pressure on the left source points while releasing pressure on the right.

During step 4 the rear hand moves into a shot-put position that fully opens the wrist source points and the points remain fully open as the arm is pushed to the front and the pressure is released from Xinshu BL-15 on the back.

Steps 5 and 6 repeat the movements of 3 and 4 but with the opposite arm.

The physical motion of the arms in steps 3, 4, 5 and 6 also stretches and loosens the ribcage to open the chest cavity and remove physical pressure on the Heart and Lungs.

DAOYIN MIND

During the Yang phase of the exercise the mental focus is on Laogong PC-8 which, in addition to "Calming the Mind" keeps the Qi flowing to the extremities. During the Yin phase of the exercise the mental focus is on the Lower Dantian to guide the Qi back.

OVERALL RESULT

The overall result is a calming action on the mind, body and spirit.[2]

Principle of Eagle Soaring in the Sky

PURPOSE

This exercise deals with the "Phlegm-Fire Disturbing Upwards" syndrome.

This exercise has the same function as "Dragon Hiding in the Blue Sea" but with the mental focus on Mingmen DU-4. The Heart is Fire in the Five Elements and the Kidneys are Water, therefore focusing on Mingmen DU-4 strengthens the Kidneys and enables Water to control Fire.

ACUPOINTS UTILIZED

The primary acupoints for "Phlegm-Fire Disturbing Upwards" used in this exercise are: Xingjian LR-2, Taichong LR-3, Yanglingquan GB-34 and Fenglong ST-40, activated by the footwork; Shaofu HT-8, Shaochong HT-9, Jianshi PC-5 and Daling PC-7, activated by the movement of the arms; Ganshu BL-18, Pishu BL-20 and Zhongwan RN-12, activated by the

---

2   "Taiji Breathing" can be combined with this exercise and "Swimming Fish Flaps Its Tail" and "Sink Qi to Dantian" to form a mini-set for regulating and calming.

torso; Fengchi GB-20, activated by the movement of the head; and Mingmen DU-4, activated by the mind.

ACTIONS DESCRIBED

Only the actions of the first two steps, the Yang or active phase, are described. Steps 3 and 4 belong to the Yin or passive phase which serves to return the body to the starting position. All other movements in the exercise are repeats.

DAOYIN FOOTWORK

The Daoyin footwork used in this exercise is Diagonal Stepping and the high resting stance. This combination of footwork serves several functions. It is used here particularly to regulate Liver-Qi through Taichong LR-3 and Yanglingquan GB-34, drain Liver-Fire through Xingjian LR-2 and resolve Phlegm through Fenglong ST-40. The Water controls Fire aspect of the footwork comes from the Kidney stimulation during the Diagonal Stepping, greatly enhanced by the high resting stance which, due to the twisting of the legs, also has a powerful effect on the Kidneys and their associated channels.

DAOYIN BODYWORK

In step 1 the movements direct the Qi to the hands with the emphasis on the little fingers to activate Shaofu HT-8 and Shaochong HT-9 to clear Heart-Fire.

During step 2, the fingers are brought to the abdomen and point to Zhongwan RN-12 and this action stimulates Jianshi PC-5 to resolve Phlegm from the Heart and Daling PC-7 to clear Heart-Fire. Zhongwan RN-12 itself can resolve Phlegm.

The physical movement of the torso in step 2 depresses the chest to expel any excess energy stuck in that area. It also acts on Ganshu BL-18 to move Liver-Qi and Pishu BL-20 to resolve

Phlegm. The turning of the head to look at the rear foot applies pressure to Fengchi GB-20 to subdue Liver-Fire.

DAOYIN MIND

During the Yang phase of the exercise the mental focus is on Mingmen DU-4, which is a significant point for the Kidneys and the Kidney energy, and during the Yin phase of the exercise the mental focus is on the Lower Dantian to guide the Qi back.

OVERALL RESULT

The overall result is to quench the Fires and remove the Phlegm.

Principle of Black Dragon Displays Talons

PURPOSE

This exercise deals with the most common stress reaction, the "Liver-Qi Stagnation turning into Fire" syndrome.

This exercise has the same function as "Swirling Clouds" but "Black Dragon Displays Its Talons" focuses on subduing Liver-Fire whereas "Swirling Clouds" is focused on regulating Liver-Qi to remove Stagnation.

ACUPOINTS UTILIZED

The primary acupoints for "Liver-Qi Stagnation turning into Fire" used in this exercise are: Xingjian LR-2, Taichong LR-3 and Yanglingquan GB-34, activated by the footwork; Shaoshang LU-11, Shangyang LI-1, Zhongchong PC-9, Guanchong SJ-1, Shaochong HT-9 and Shaoze SI-1, activated by spreading the fingers; Zhangmen LR-13, Qimen LR-14 and Ganshu BL-18, activated by the movement of the torso; and Xingjian LR-2, reinforced by the mind and physical pressure.

ACTIONS DESCRIBED

Only the actions of the first three steps, the Yang or active phase, are described. Steps 7 and 8 are the Yin or passive phase which serves to return the body to the starting position. All other movements in the exercise are repeats.

DAOYIN FOOTWORK

The Daoyin footwork used in this exercise is Side Stepping and the low resting stance. This combination of footwork serves several functions. It is used here particularly to regulate Liver-Qi through Taichong LR-3 and Yanglingquan GB-34 and to subdue Liver-Fire through Xingjian LR-2. Moving into and out of the low resting stance strongly stimulates the Kidneys and their associated channels which enables the Kidneys to nourish the Liver.

DAOYIN BODYWORK

In step 1 the backward and upward movement of the arms physically opens the rib cage to create more space in the upper abdomen to allow the Liver to expand. In step two the rib cage is returned to the normal position which applies pressure to the Liver, the net result being a pumping action which initiates Liver-Qi movement.

During step 2, after the body squats into the low resting stance one side of the chest is compressed and the other side expanded. This acts on Ganshu BL-18 to remove Stagnation, and also on Zhangmen LR-13 and Qimen LR-14 to regulate Liver-Qi. At the same time, pressure is applied with the thumb to Xingjian LR-2 to subdue Liver-Fire.

Step 3 brings energy to the hands and spreading the fingers wide stimulates the points at the fingertips, causing the Qi to be distributed throughout the system, thus encouraging a smooth flow of Qi.

DAOYIN MIND

During the Yang phase of the exercise the mental focus is on Xingjian LR-2, which is a significant point to subdue Liver-Fire, and during the Yin phase of the exercise the mental focus is on the Lower Dantian to guide the Qi back.

OVERALL RESULT

The overall result is to subdue Liver-Fire, regulate Liver-Qi and remove Stagnation.

Principle of Dragon Hiding in the Blue Sea

PURPOSE

This exercise deals with the "Phlegm-Fire Disturbing Upwards" syndrome.

This exercise has the same function as "Eagle Soaring in the Sky" but with the mental focus on Laogong PC-8. In Daoyin theory Laogong PC-8 is one of the main points for working on the Heart.

ACUPOINTS UTILIZED

The primary acupoints for "Phlegm-Fire Disturbing Upwards" used in the exercise are: Xingjian LR-2, Taichong LR-3, Yanglingquan GB-34 and Fenglong ST-40, activated by the footwork; Shaofu HT-8, Shaochong HT-9, Jianshi PC-5 and Daling PC-7, activated by the movement of the arms; Fengchi GB-20, activated by the movement of the head; and Laogong PC-8, activated by the mind.

ACTIONS DESCRIBED

Only the actions of the first two steps, the Yang or active phase, are described. Steps 3 and 4 belong to the Yin or passive phase which serves to return the body to the starting position. All other movements in the exercise are repeats.

DAOYIN FOOTWORK

The Daoyin footwork used in this exercise is Side Stepping and the low resting stance. This combination of footwork serves several functions. It is used here particularly to regulate Liver-Qi through Taichong LR-3 and Yanglingquan GB-34, drain Liver-Fire through Xingjian LR-2 and resolve Phlegm through Fenglong ST-40. The Water controls Fire aspect of the footwork comes from the Kidney stimulation in the low resting stance which has an even greater effect on the Kidneys and their associated channels than the high resting stance.

DAOYIN BODYWORK

In step 1 the movements direct the Qi to the hands with the emphasis on the little fingers to activate Shaofu HT-8 and Shaochong HT-9 to clear Heart-Fire.

During step 2, the hands are hyperextended which affects Jianshi PC-5 to eliminate Phlegm from the Heart and to open the three source points at the wrist fully, of which the important one for this exercise is Daling PC-7, to clear Heart-Fire.

DAOYIN MIND

During the Yang phase of the exercise the mental focus is on Laogong PC-8, which is a very effective point for draining Heart-Fire, and during the Yin phase of the exercise the mental focus is on the Lower Dantian to guide the Qi back.

OVERALL RESULT

The overall result is to quench the Fires and remove the Phlegm.

Principle of Swirling Clouds

PURPOSE

This exercise deals with the most common stress reaction, the "Liver-Qi Stagnation turning into Fire" syndrome.

This exercise has the same function as "Black Dragon Displays Its Talons" but "Swirling Clouds" focuses on regulating Liver-Qi to remove Stagnation whereas "Black Dragon Displays Its Talons" is focused on subduing Liver-Fire.

ACUPOINTS UTILIZED

The primary acupoints for "Liver-Qi Stagnation turning into Fire" used in this exercise are: Xingjian LR-2, Taichong LR-3, Yanglingquan GB-34 and Zuqiaoyin GB-44 activated by the footwork; Neiguan PC-6 and Zhigou SJ-6 activated by the arm movement; Zhangmen LR-13 and Qimen LR-14 activated by the movement of the torso; and Neiguan PC-6, reinforced by the mind.

ACTIONS DESCRIBED

Only the actions of the first three steps, the Yang or active phase, are described. Step 8 is the Yin or passive phase which serves to return the body to the starting position. All other movements in the exercise are repeats.

DAOYIN FOOTWORK

The Daoyin footwork used in this exercise is Side Stepping, horse stance and side bow stance. This combination of footwork serves several functions. It is used here particularly to regulate Liver-Qi through Taichong LR-3 and Yanglingquan GB-34 and to subdue Liver-Fire through Xingjian LR-2. Both Yanglingquan GB-34 acupoints are strongly activated in the horse stance while the side bow stance uses Zuqiaoyin GB-44 to subdue Liver-Yang.

DAOYIN BODYWORK

In step 1 the sideways and upward movement of the arms brings the Qi to the hands and also physically opens the rib cage to create more space in the upper abdomen which allows the Liver to expand.

During step 2, the arms come together until Neiguan PC-6 and Zhigou SJ-6 are pressed against each other to activate their regulating Liver-Qi functions. This also closes the rib cage which applies pressure to the Liver.

Step 3 releases all the pressures and brings the body back into a preparatory position, with the rib cage open to ease the Liver, ready for the repeat actions. Each opening and closing of the ribs has a massaging action on the Liver.

DAOYIN MIND

During the Yang phase of the exercise the physical action on Neiguan PC-6 is bolstered by the mental focus on the point to enhance the regulation of Liver-Qi, and during the Yin phase of the exercise the mental focus is on the Lower Dantian to guide the Qi back.

OVERALL RESULT

The overall result is the regulation of Liver-Qi to remove Stagnation and to subdue Liver-Fire.

Principle of Swimming Fish Flaps Its Tail

PURPOSE

This exercise deals with the "Disturbance of the Mind" syndrome.

This exercise has the same function as "Swirling Water" but "Swimming Fish Flaps Its Tail" is of a Yin nature compared to the Yang nature of "Swirling Water." These movements have a more meditative effect in their rhythmic motion.

ACUPOINTS UTILIZED

The primary acupoints for "Calming the Mind" used in this exercise are: Yongquan KI-1, Taixi KI-3, Yinbai SP-1, Taichong LR-3 and Jiexi ST-41, activated by the footwork; Shenmen HT-7, Daling PC-7, Jiuwei RN-15 and Hegu LI-4, activated by movements of the arms and torso; and Laogong PC-8, activated by the mind.

ACTIONS DESCRIBED

Only the actions of the first two steps, the Yang or active phase, are described. Steps 7 and 8 belong to the Yin or passive phase, which serves to return the body to the starting position. All other movements in the exercise are repeats.

DAOYIN FOOTWORK

The footwork used throughout this exercise is the Daoyin Diagonal Stepping and the weight-shift from bow stance to toe-up stance. This footwork serves several functions. It is used here particularly for its stimulation of Yinbai SP-1, Taichong LR-3, Yongquan KI-1, Taixi KI-3 and Jiexi ST-41 which together have a powerful calming effect on the mind. It also acts on Yinqiao mai and Yangqiao mai to regulate the Yin and Yang balance in the body.

DAOYIN BODYWORK

In step 1, swinging the arms backward and upward physically opens up the chest to enhance the breathing and restrict Qi flow up Dumai, directing it instead up Renmai to Jiuwei RN-15.

During steps 2 to 6 the weight-shifting, torso turning and sweeping the arms back and forth results in a soothing, rhythmic action which strongly stimulates the parasympathetic nervous system, thus enhancing the calming actions of the Hegu LI-4 alignment with Jiuwei RN-15.

DAOYIN MIND

During the Yang phase of the exercise the mental focus is on Laogong PC-8, which in addition to "Calming the Mind" keeps the Qi flowing to the extremities, and during the Yin phase of the exercise the mental focus is on the Lower Dantian to guide the Qi back.

OVERALL RESULT

The overall result is a calming action on the mind, body and spirit.[3]

Stress Prevention Principles of Action

The structure of the Stress Prevention routine

The routine consists of eight exercises grouped into four sections.

Section 1	1. Taiji Breathing	Opening
Section 2	2. Round Fan Covers the Moon	Water controls Fire
	3. Buffalo Ploughs the Land	Fire controls Metal
	4. Distinguished Lord Combs Hair	Metal controls Wood
	5. Flower Displays Buddha	Wood controls Earth
	6. One Hands Supports Heaven	Earth controls Water
Section 3	7. Tapping Rendu	Connects and balances
Section 4	8. Sink Qi to Dantian	Closing

---

3 "Taiji Breathing" and "Swirling Water" can be combined with this exercise and "Sink Qi to Dantian" to form a mini-set for regulating and calming.

The purpose of Section 1 is to prepare the body and mind for the Yang, active exercises to follow.

The purpose of Section 2 is to take control of the mental and emotional states by following the Controlling Cycle of the Five Elements (see Appendix A).

The purpose of Section 3 is to establish openings to connect the Yin and Yang channels to their respective reservoirs to help maintain an energy balance.

The purpose of Section 4 is to return the body and mind back to a Yin, peaceful state.

Exercises 1, "Taiji Breathing" and 8, "Sink Qi to Dantian" are common to the Stress Relief routine as well and have already been described.

The principles of Stress Prevention Exercises 2 to 7 are described below. These exercises are designed to work with stage 1 of the chronic stress situation, the "onset" or mental, spiritual and emotional response.

Clearly, the mental and emotional responses are not confined to the "onset" phase. In chronic stress these responses are continuous but their trigger is at the onset. The emotions themselves are not a problem; it is the extremes of the emotions that cause problems. An example is the violent outburst of anger when the Liver is at one extreme and the suppression of anger at the other extreme.

The exercises in this routine are crafted to bring about an emotional, spiritual and mental balance and then, with regular practice, to build a defence against the stressor to prevent further onset.

Principle of Round Fan Covers the Moon

PURPOSE

Emotionally the Kidneys are related to fear and the mental/ spiritual aspect is willpower. Fear robs us of our willpower.

The purpose of this exercise is to create a mental, spiritual and emotional balance in the Kidney system which, in turn, can prevent the Heart functions from becoming extreme (in the Five Element theory this is called Water controls Fire).

ACUPOINTS UTILIZED

The primary acupoints for "Water controlling Fire" used in this exercise are: Dadun LR-1, Yinbai SP-1, Yongquan KI-1 and Taixi Ki-3, activated by the footwork; Shaoshang LU-11, Shangyang LI-1, Zhongchong PC-9, Guanchong SJ-1, Shaochong HT-9 and Shaoze SI-1, activated by flicking the fingers; Shenshu BL-23, activated by turning the body; and Mingmen DU-4, activated by the mind.

ACTIONS DESCRIBED

Only the actions of the first two steps, the Yang or active phase, are described. Steps 3 and 4 are the Yin or passive phase which serves to return the body to the starting position. All other movements in the exercise are repeats.

DAOYIN FOOTWORK

The Daoyin footwork used in this exercise is Side Stepping, Crossover Stepping and the high resting stance. This combination of footwork serves several functions but it is used here particularly to build up to the strong Kidney stimulation through Yongquan KI-1 and Taixi Ki-3 and the "wringing" action on the channel. There is also a small effect on the Spleen and Liver through Yinbai SP-1 and Dadun LR-1 during the Side Stepping.

DAOYIN BODYWORK

In step 1, bringing the hands back-to-back closes the source points on the wrists which increases the Qi pressure. After the hands are raised, the source points are opened when the fingers are rolled to push the fingernails against each other to create a surge of high pressure Qi which, combined with the flicking action, gives strong stimulation to the acupoints on the fingertips causing the Qi to be distributed throughout the entire system.

After the flick the hands are separated to open the chest to allow the lungs to fill properly.

During step 2 the twisting movement of the body aids the "wringing" action on the Kidney channel and also applies physical pressure to massage the Kidney and activate Shenshu BL-23.

The movement of the thumbs from closed palms to open palms also stimulates the Lung energy.

DAOYIN MIND

During the Yang phase of the exercise the mental focus is on Mingmen DU-4, which is a significant point for the Kidneys and the Kidney energy, and during the Yin phase of the exercise the mental focus is on the Lower Dantian to guide the Qi back.

OVERALL RESULT

The overall result is an action on the Kidneys to reduce fear and enhance willpower which, in turn, can have a positive effect on the joy in the Heart.

Principle of Buffalo Ploughs Land

PURPOSE

Emotionally the Heart is related to joy and the mental/spiritual aspect is spirit. Lack of joy certainly damps the spirit.

The purpose of this exercise is to create a mental, spiritual and emotional balance in the Heart system which, in turn, can prevent the Lung functions from becoming extreme (in the Five Element theory this is called Fire controls Metal).

ACUPOINTS UTILIZED

The primary acupoints for "Fire controlling Metal" used in this exercise are: Yongquan KI-1 and Taixi KI-3, activated by the footwork; Shenmen HT-7, Shaofu HT-8, Shaochong HT-9 and Daling PC-7, activated by the arm movement; Laogong PC-8, activated by the mind.

ACTIONS DESCRIBED

Only the actions of the first two steps, the Yang or active phase, are described. Step 8 is the Yin or passive phase which serves to return the body to the starting position. All other movements in the exercise are repeats.

DAOYIN FOOTWORK

The Daoyin footwork used in this exercise is Diagonal Stepping and the weight-shift from bow stance to toe-up stance. This combination of footwork serves several functions. It is used here particularly to stimulate the Kidneys through Yongquan KI-1 and Taixi KI-3. There is also a small effect on the Spleen and Liver through Yinbai Sp-1 and Dadun LR-1 during the Diagonal Stepping.

DAOYIN BODYWORK

In step 1, raising the arms up the front directs Qi to the hands with the emphasis on the little fingers to activate the Heart points Shaofu HT-8 and Shaochong HT-9.

During step 2 bringing the hands inward closes Shenmen HT-7 and Daling PC-7 which increases their Qi pressure and lowering them gradually opens the points to release the pressure gently.

Step 1 and step 2 physically keep the chest sunk to stop energy moving into the Heart and Lungs too soon.

DAOYIN MIND

During the Yang phase of the exercise the mental focus is on Laogong PC-8 which, in Qigong, is one of the most significant points for the Heart, and during the Yin phase of the exercise the mental focus is on the Lower Dantian to guide the Qi back.

OVERALL RESULT

The overall result is an action on the Heart to encourage happiness and lift the spirits which, in turn, can have a positive effect on the sadness in the Lungs.

Principle of Distinguished Lord Combs Hair

PURPOSE

Emotionally the Lungs are related to sadness and the mental/spiritual aspect is the Corporeal Soul. Sadness leads to a lack of feelings and sensations as the Corporeal Soul governs these actions.

The purpose of this exercise is to create a mental, spiritual and emotional balance in the Lung system which, in turn, can prevent the Liver functions from becoming extreme (in the Five Element theory this is called Metal controls Wood).

ACUPOINTS UTILIZED

The primary acupoints for "Metal controlling Wood" used in this exercise are: Yinbai SP-1, Dadun LR-1, and the three source points Taibai SP-3, Taixi KI-3 and Taichong LR-3, activated by the footwork; Feishu BL-13 and Dabao SP-21 activated by the body; Hegu LI-4, Shaoshang LU-11 and Shangyang LI-1 and the three source points Shenmen HT-7, Daling PC-7 and Taiyuan LU-9 activated by the hands; Shangyang LI-1 is also activated by the mind.

ACTIONS DESCRIBED

Only the actions of the first two steps, the Yang or active phase, are described. Steps 7 and 8 are the Yin or passive phase which serves to return the body to the starting position. All other movements in the exercise are repeats.

DAOYIN FOOTWORK

The Daoyin footwork used in this exercise is Side Stepping and the horse stance. This combination of footwork serves several functions. It is used here particularly to strengthen the Spleen through Yinbai SP-1 and Taibai SP-3 which nourish the Lungs, and to strengthen the Liver, the target of the Lung control, through Dadun LR-1 and Taichong LR-3. The horse stance itself acts through Yanglingquan GB-34 on the Liver and through Taixi KI-3 on the Kidneys to nourish the Liver.

DAOYIN BODYWORK

In step 1 the raising of the arms opens the chest and aids breathing while placing the hand behind the head closes one side of the chest and keeps the other open which has an effect on Dabao SP-21, aiding energetically in the opening, and on Feishu BL-13, back transporting point which has a direct effect on the Lungs.

During step 2 one hand is changed into an eight character palm, which has a very strong Lung effect through Taiyuan LU-9, Lung source point, Shaoshang LU-11, Shangyang LI-1 and Hegu LI-4, Large Intestine source point.

The source points Shenmen HT-7 and Daling PC-7 are also fully opened but with the fingers bent their effects are lessened.

DAOYIN MIND

During the Yang phase of the exercise the mental focus is on Shangyang LI-1 which, in Qigong, is an alternate point of focus to Shaoshang LU-1, as it is the next point along in the energy circuit, and during the Yin phase of the exercise the mental focus is on the Lower Dantian to guide the Qi back.

OVERALL RESULT

The overall result is an action on the Lungs to remove sadness and lead to a return of feelings and sensation which, in turn, can have a positive effect on frustration and anger in the Liver.

Principle of Flower Displays Buddha

PURPOSE

Emotionally the Liver is related to frustration and anger and the mental/spiritual aspect is the Ethereal Soul. Frustration and anger lead to disturbance of the Ethereal Soul which has a governing action over our mental balance.

The purpose of this exercise is to create a mental, spiritual and emotional balance in the Liver system which, in turn, can prevent the Spleen functions from becoming extreme (in the Five Element theory this is called Wood controls Earth).

ACUPOINTS UTILIZED

The primary acupoints for "Wood controlling Earth" used in this exercise are: Yongquan KI-1, Taixi KI-3, Dadun LR-1 and Taichong LR-3, activated by the footwork; Zhangmen LR-13, Qimen LR-14, Riyue GB-24, Jingmen GB-25, activated by the body; Laogong PC-8, Shaoshang LU-11, Shangyang LI-1, Zhongchong PC-9, Guanchong SJ-1, Shaochong HT-9 and Shaoze SI-1, activated by the hands.

ACTIONS DESCRIBED

Only the actions of the first three steps, the Yang or active phase, are described. Step 8 is the Yin or passive phase which serves to return the body to the starting position. All other movements in the exercise are repeats.

DAOYIN FOOTWORK

The Daoyin footwork used in this exercise is Diagonal Stepping and the weight-shift from twisted bow stance to toe-up stance. This combination of footwork serves several functions. It is used here particularly to stimulate the Kidneys through Yongquan KI-1 and Taixi KI-3 in order to nourish the Liver, and to stimulate the Liver through Dadun LR-1 and Taichong LR-3. The twisted bow stance increases the effects through Taichong LR-3.

DAOYIN BODYWORK

In step 1 the palms are drawn up the body until Laogong PC-8 connects with Qimen LR-14. This guides the Qi from the Lower Dantian to these Liver points and to the palms of the hands.

During step 2 as the hands are raised the forearms give a light massage stroke to the Liver channel from Zhangmen LR-13 to Qimen LR-14 to encourage Qi flow through the Liver channel. This step concludes with the fingers spread wide to activate the fingertip acupoints to disperse energy through the system. Here also, the eyes, the sense organs of the Liver, are opened wide.

Step 3 changes the hands into shang fists which presses Shangyang LI-1 and Shaoshang LU-11 together, giving a strong Lung stimulus and as the arms are lowered the forearms give a light massage stroke to the Gallbladder channel from Riyue GB-24 to Jingmen GB-25 which are influential points for the Liver.

DAOYIN MIND

During the Yang phase of the exercise the mental focus is on the tigermouth to help stimulate the dispersal of Qi through the fingertips, and during the Yin phase of the exercise the mental focus is on the Lower Dantian to guide the Qi back.

OVERALL RESULT

The overall result is an action on the Liver to remove anger and frustration, to settle the disturbance of the Ethereal Soul and to recover our mental equilibrium.

Principle of One Hand Supports Heaven

PURPOSE

Emotionally the Spleen is related to anxiety and the mental/ spiritual aspect is the intellect. Anxiety prevents us from thinking clearly.

The purpose of this exercise is to create a mental, spiritual and emotional balance in the Spleen system which, in turn, can prevent the Kidney functions from becoming extreme (in the Five Element theory this is called Earth controls Water).

ACUPOINTS UTILIZED

The primary acupoints for "Earth controlling Water" used in this exercise are: Yinbai SP-1, Taibai SP-3 and Taixi KI-3, activated by the footwork; Shenmen HT-7, Daling PC-7 and Taiyuan LU-9, activated by the hands; Zhangmen LR-13 and Dabao SP-21, activated by the body.

ACTIONS DESCRIBED

Only the actions of the first two steps, the Yang or active phase, are described. Steps 3 and 4 are the Yin or passive phase which serves to return the body to the starting position. All other movements in the exercise are repeats.

DAOYIN FOOTWORK

The Daoyin footwork used in this exercise is Side Stepping and the horse stance. This combination of footwork serves several functions. It is used here particularly to strengthen the Spleen through Yinbai SP-1 and Taibai SP-3 while Side Stepping and during the horse stance there is an action on the Kidneys, the target of the Spleen control, through Taixi KI-3.

DAOYIN BODYWORK

In step 1 the raising of the hands guides the Qi up the Dumai channel to Dazhui DU-14 ready to branch into the arms.

During step 2 the Qi flows into the arms and the wrist source points, Shenmen HT-7, Daling PC-7 and Taiyuan LU-9, are opened to allow increased flow in order to influence the Heart, which thereby nourishes the Spleen, and also to influence the Lungs, which thereby nourish the Kidneys, the object of the Spleen control.

The side bend of the body applies pressure to Zhangmen LR-13 to strengthen the Spleen and to open Dabao SP-21 which is a significant point not just for the Spleen but for the whole body.

DAOYIN MIND

During both the Yang and Yin phases of the exercise the mental focus is on the Lower Dantian. In Daoyin the Lower Dantian is not only the main energy reservoir; it is also the reflex point for the Spleen, one of the Five Pulses.[4] During the Yang phase its

---

4   The Five Pulses are the two palms of the hands, the two soles of the feet and the Lower Dantian and refers to the pulsing of Qi through the body. The Lower Dantian is related to the Spleen, the palms to the Heart and Lungs while the soles are related to the Liver and Kidneys.

action is on the Spleen and in the Yin phase its action is on the energy reservoir.

OVERALL RESULT

The overall result is an action on the Spleen to ease anxiety and allow clarity of thought.

Principle of Tapping Rendu

PURPOSE

The purpose of this exercise is to normalize the Qi in the Yin and Yang channels.

ACUPOINTS UTILIZED

The only acupoints for "Normalizing the Qi" used in this exercise are Mingmen DU-4 and Jiuwei RN-15 activated by the tapping, and Dazhui DU-14 activated by turning the head.

ACTIONS DESCRIBED

Only the actions of the first step, the Yang or active phase, are described. Step 8 in Part 2 is the Yin or passive phase which serves to return the body to the starting position. All other movements in the exercise are repeats.

DAOYIN FOOTWORK

The only Daoyin footwork used in this exercise is Side Stepping and it is used here solely to step into position.

DAOYIN BODYWORK

The front hand taps Jiuwei RN-15 which is a source point for all five Yin organs (Liver, Heart, Spleen, Lungs and Kidneys) and stimulates the connection between the Qi in the regular Yin channels and the energy stored in the extraordinary channels.

Turning the head activates Dazhui DU-14 which is a connecting point for all the Yang channels and can help to harmonize the energy in those channels.

All the extraordinary channels are directly or indirectly connected to the Kidneys and the Jing or Essence. The rear hand tapping Mingmen DU-4 stimulates the Kidneys and the Essence and, therefore, influences the extraordinary channels.

DAOYIN MIND

During the Yang phase of the exercise the mental focus is on the points being tapped, namely Mingmen DU-4 and Jiuwei RN-15 to reinforce the tapping action, and during the Yin phase of the exercise the mental focus is on the Lower Dantian to guide the Qi back.

OVERALL RESULT

The overall result is an action that normalizes the energy levels in all the channels.[5]

---

5   Regular channels are like rivers and streams for the energy while the extra channels are like lakes and reservoirs. Excess in regular channels should be transferred into the extraordinary channels but if the regular channels are low then more energy can be released from the extraordinary channels.

Appendix A:
Five Elements (Wuxing)

The Wuxing or Five Element theory is a vast subject (the entire universe can be divided into five categories) so here we limit ourselves to those aspects of the theory that relate to Qigong and stress as discussed in this book.

Wuxing, more correctly, is concerned with five dynamic processes or phases of activity rather than elements which implies something fixed. However, as the name "Five Elements" has become commonplace we will continue to use it here.

Yin and Yang are not absolutes; they are relational and that relationship changes according to what two things are being compared. For example, if Yang is hard and Yin is soft then my hand is Yang compared to the Yin air surrounding it but my hand is also Yin compared to a Yang block of granite, therefore my hand is Yin and Yang simultaneously.

This idea of changing relationships is also at the heart of the Five Elements, only now we are comparing the aspects of five things instead of two. A quick check of various texts on the Five Elements reveals what appear to be inconsistencies and sometimes complete contradictions but we have to remember that there are no absolutes here, only relationships.

These Five Elements show the natural recurring cycles and the ebb and flow of energies in everything. This theory was first systematized by Zou Yen (circa. 350–270 BC) but, as the system follows the Daoist truism which states "change is the only constant," it is an unfinished work. It is unfinished and will continue to be incomplete because it seeks to discover the dynamic relationships between a myriad of ever changing situations and objects.

It is useful to view the Five Elements as blank templates into which various items can be dropped in order to see the relationships that exist between them.

Here, with echoes of the Introduction, we come full circle to see that the Five Element templates are specific but the contents non-specific.

In Table 1 some of the possible correspondences are listed. When these are inserted into any of the three Five Element diagrams we can now see the relationships that exist between these things.

Table 1: Five Element Correspondences

	Wood	Fire	Earth	Metal	Water
Yin organ	Liver	Heart	Spleen	Lungs	Kidney
Yang organ	Gallbladder	Small Intestine	Stomach	Large Intestine	Bladder
Tissue	Tendons	Blood vessels	Muscle	Skin	Bones
Opening	Eyes	Tongue	Mouth	Nose	Ears
Sense	Sight	Taste	Touch	Smell	Hearing
Emotion	Anger	Joy	Anxiety	Sadness	Fear
Negativity	Hostility	Greed	Ambition	Stubborn	Desire
Voice	Shouting	Laughing	Singing	Crying	Groaning
Taste	Sour	Bitter	Sweet	Spicy	Salty
Direction	East	South	Centre	West	North
Colour	Green	Red	Yellow	White	Blue
Climate	Wind	Heat	Damp	Dry	Cold
Mind	Rational	Spiritual	Tranquil	Sentimental	Desire
Morality	Benevolence	Humility	Trusting	Rectitude	Wisdom
Phase	New Yang	Full Yang	Balance	New Yin	Full Yin
Spirit	Spirit	Conscience	Thought	Instinct	Will

In the Generating cycle it can be seen that Wood generates Fire, Fire generates Earth, Earth generates Metal, Metal generates Water and Water generates Wood bringing us full circle. (Diagram 3)

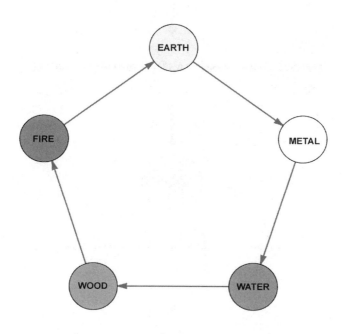

Diagram 3: Five Element Generating Cycle

Another way of looking at this is Wood is the mother of Fire and Fire is the son of Wood so in the generating cycle the mother nourishes the son, known as the Mother–Son Law.

Cruciform arrangement can be used to highlight the balancing actions of Fire and Water and of Metal and Wood with the Earth being a pivotal point. (Diagram 4) This is expanded upon in the pentagonal arrangement of the Controlling Cycle (Diagram 5) which is used as the method of regulation in the Stress Prevention routine.

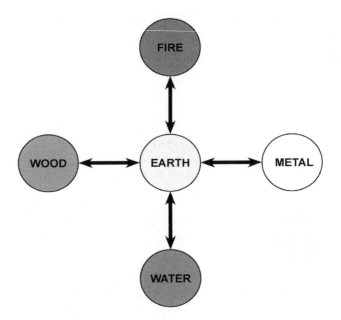

Diagram 4: Five Element Cruciform Arrangement

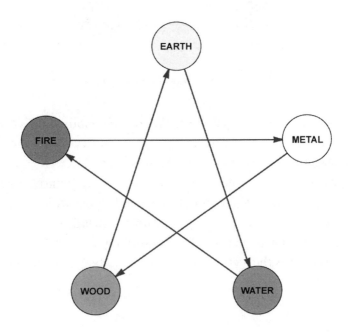

Diagram 5: Five Element Controlling Cycle

For example, in the Stress Prevention routine the exercises are performed specifically in the Controlling Cycle sequence and that template is filled with the correspondences of the internal organs, emotions and spirit. Therefore, Water (Kidneys, fear and willpower) has controlling actions on Fire (Heart, joy and conscience) which has controlling actions on Metal (Lungs, sadness and instinct) which has controlling actions on Wood (Liver, anger and spirit) which has controlling actions on Earth (Spleen, anxiety and thought) which completes the cycle by having controlling actions on Water.

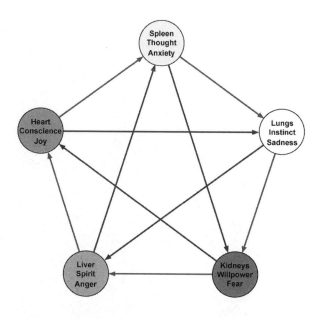

Diagram 6: Five Element Correspondences

Diagram 6 shows the combined template of the Controlling and Generating cycles with some of the correspondences relating to stress. Stress can block change but all things *should* change and the Five Elements allow us to understand the nature of the process and where that process is blocked.

Appendix B:
Energy System

The energy system of the human body is very complex and Traditional Chinese Medicine utilizes a large part of the system diagnostically but generally concerns itself only with the channels and collaterals when it comes to treatment. Qigong expands on this and includes the core of the energy system, the Dantians (Cinnabar Fields), the areas where energy is collected, transformed and circulated.

The energy of the human body is distributed throughout the system by a series of channels and collaterals which link the internal organs with the various tissues and organs of the superficial area of the body to make an organic integrity. In this network the channels are the main trunks which pertain to the respective internal organs, while the collaterals are their minor branches distributed throughout the body. This network provides communication, regulation and distribution.

The human body is a complex system that contains many parts that must communicate with each other in order to function harmoniously and it is the channel system that provides the means of communication. In the Five Element (Wuxing) system it is seen that the internal organs have controlling action on each other and this mutual regulation is provided by the orderly flow of Qi through the channel network. As the energy channels are spread throughout the body so they form a distribution network to supply all parts of the body with nutrients and fluids driven by channel Qi.

The main part of the energy system consists of the Twelve Regular Channels, the Eight Extra Channels and the Fifteen Collaterals. The Twelve Regular Channels, together with Renmai and Dumai of the Eight Extra Channels, form the Fourteen Channels, which are the only channels to possess acupoints of their own.

The Twelve Regular Channels run lengthwise through the body and each channel is designated a Yin or a Yang channel depending on the Yin or Yang internal organ it connects with. Also, each Yang channel has a secondary relationship with a Yin organ and each Yin channel has a secondary relationship with a Yang organ.

Each regular channel connects with another regular channel to form an energy circuit that takes 24 hours to complete and runs in the following order: Lung, Large Intestine, Stomach, Spleen, Heart, Small Intestine, Bladder, Kidneys, Pericardium, Sanjiao (Triple Heater), Gallbladder and Liver. Each channel peaks, or is more active than the rest, during the two-hour period associated with it.

If the energy does not flow smoothly in the correct direction through the channels the whole circuit becomes jeopardized and health problems emerge. (For a good description of the channel system see *The Essential Book of TCM: Vol 1 Theory* by Liu Yanchi, Columbia University Press.)

In addition to the channel system, Qigong practice utilizes three Dantians, the Upper Dantian, which is connected with spirit (Shen), the Middle Dantian, which is connected with energy (Qi) and the Lower Dantian, which is connected with essence (Jing).

The Upper Dantian is located inside the head, between the eyebrows. This area corresponds to consciousness, spirit and generally, all mental functioning. The Middle Dantian is located in the heart (although some alternate sources place it at the solar plexus). This deals primarily with health of the internal organs and respiration. The Lower Dantian is generally considered to be the primary energy storage area of the body. When people speak of the Dantian they are usually referring to the Lower Dantian. The Lower Dantian corresponds to physical vitality and to sexual health and energy. In particular, it is the place to which energy is brought to after Qigong exercise.

Please see the meridian charts on the following pages for a visual representation of the channels.

The Twelve Regular Channels

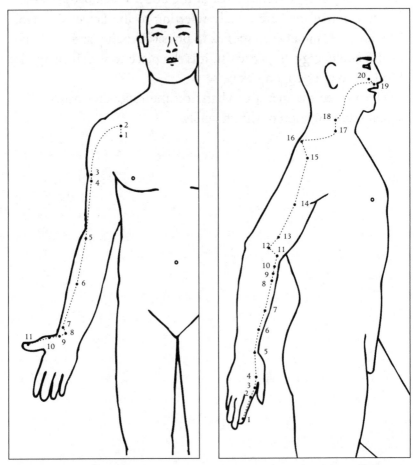

Lung Channel (LU)   Large Intestine Channel (LI)

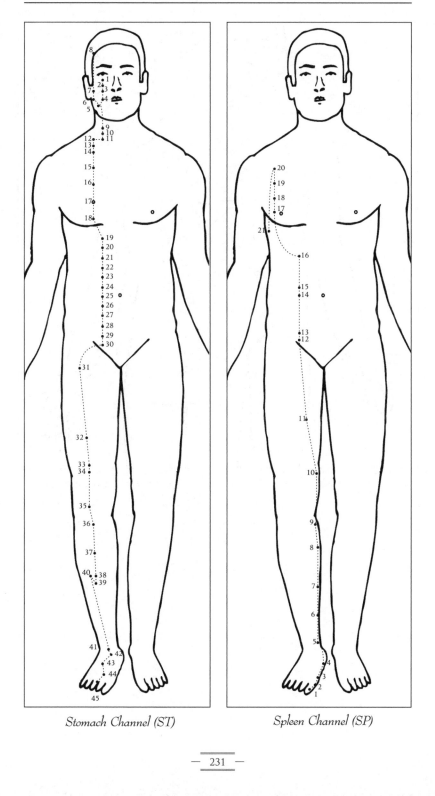

Stomach Channel (ST)   *Spleen Channel (SP)*

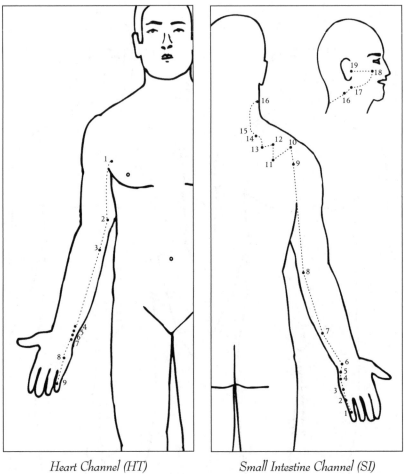

Heart Channel (HT)   Small Intestine Channel (SI)

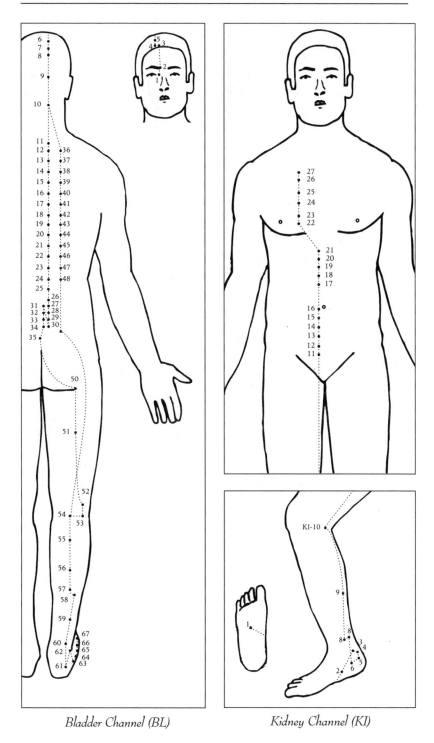

Bladder Channel (BL)

Kidney Channel (KI)

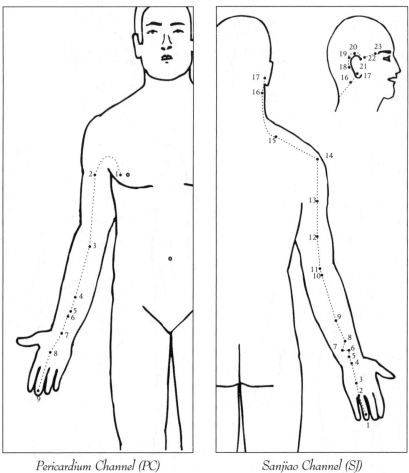

Pericardium Channel (PC)   Sanjiao Channel (SJ)

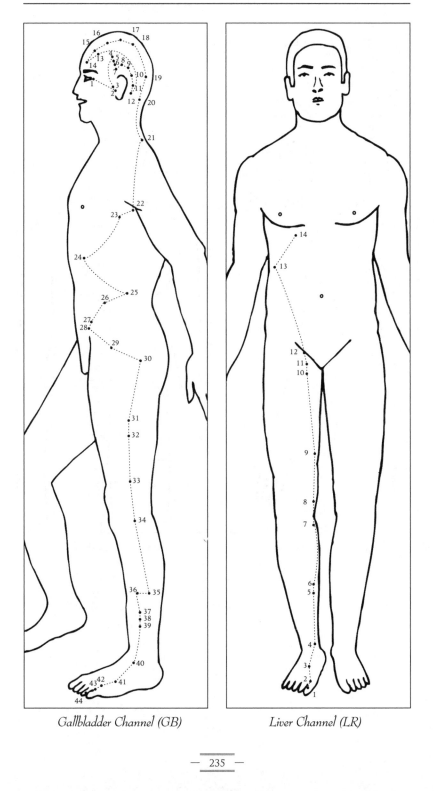

Gallbladder Channel (GB)   *Liver Channel (LR)*

The Eight Extra Channels

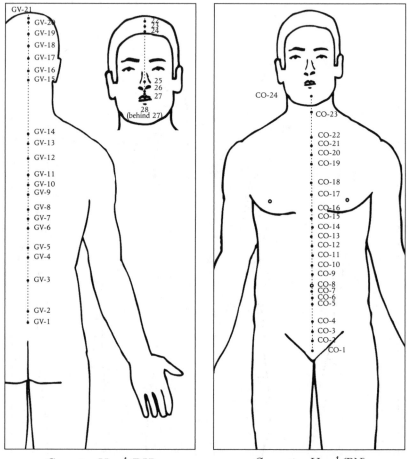

Governing Vessel (DU)   *Conception Vessel (RN)*

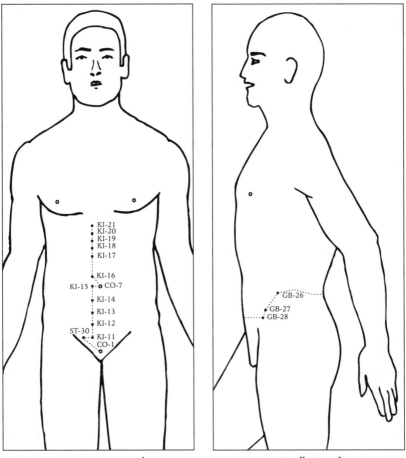

Penetrating Vessel   *Girdle Vessel*

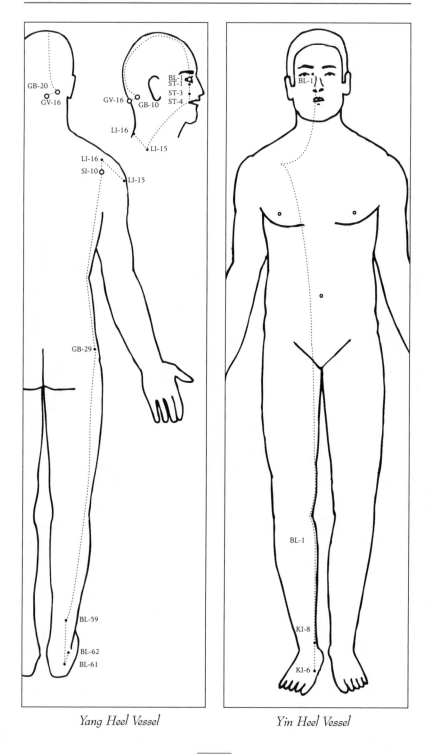

GB-20
GV-16

GV-16
GB-10

BL-1
ST-1
ST-3
ST-4

LI-16

LI-15

LI-16
SI-10
LI-15

BL-1

GB-29

BL-59

BL-62
BL-61

BL-1

KI-8

KI-6

Yang Heel Vessel

Yin Heel Vessel

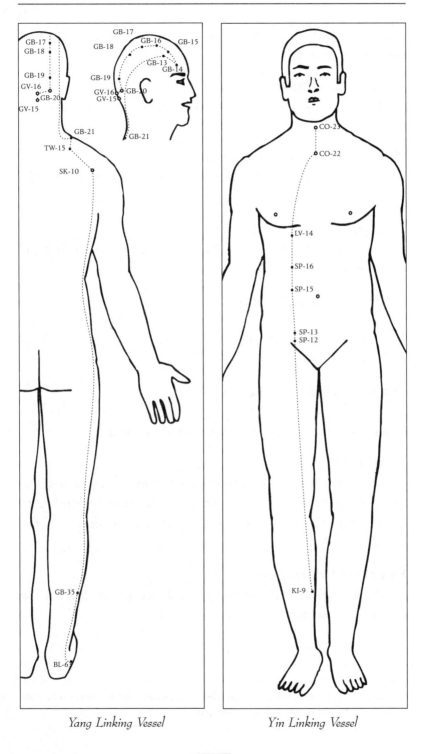

Yang Linking Vessel　　　　*Yin Linking Vessel*

Listed below are acupoints mentioned in this book with a brief description of their locations.

Taiyuan LU-9 (Source Point)
At the transverse crease of the wrist, in the depression of the radial side of the radial artery.

Shaoshang LU-11 (Well Point)
On the radial side of the thumb, 0.1 cun[1] posterior from the corner of the fingernail.

Shangyang LI-1 (Well Point)
On the radial side of the index finger, 0.1 cun posterior from the corner of the nail.

Hegu LI-4 (Source Point)
On the dorsum of the hand, between the first and second metacarpal bones, at the midpoint of the second metacarpal bone on the radial side.

Fenglong ST-40 (Connecting Point)
8 cun superior and anterior to the lateral malleolus, and two finger-breadths from the anterior crest of the tibia.

Jiexi ST-41
In the central depression of the crease between the instep of the foot and leg, between the tendons of muscles extensor digitorum longus and extersor hallucis longus, level with the tip of the lateral malleolus.

Yinbai SP-1 (Well Point)
On the medial side of the big toe, 0.1 cun posterior from the corner of the toenail.

---

1   Cun: A measurement used in acupuncture that is proportional to a person's body. It is the width of a person's thumb at the knuckle.

Taibai SP-3 (Source Point)

On the medial border of the foot, in the depression of the junction of the red and white skin, proximal and inferior to the first metatarsophalangeal joint.

Dabao SP-21 (Connecting Point)

On the lateral side of the chest, on the midaxillary line, in the sixth intercostal space. 6 cun below the axilla, midway between the axilla and the free end of the eleventh rib.

Shenmen HT-7 (Source Point)

On the transverse crease of the wrist, in the depression in the radial side of the tendon of the ulnar flexor muscle of the wrist.

Shaofu HT-8

On the palm, between the fourth and fifth metacarpal bones, where the tip of the little finger rests when a fist is made.

Shaochong HT-9 (Well Point)

On the radial side of the little finger, 0.1 cun posterior from the corner of the fingernail.

Shaoze SI-1 (Well Point)

On the ulnar side of the little finger, 0.1 cun posterior from the corner of the fingernail.

Feishu BL-13 (Transporting Point)

On the back, below the spinous process of the third thoracic vertebra, 1.5 cun lateral to the posterior midline.

Xinshu BL-15 (Transporting Point)

On the back, below the spinous process of the fifth thoracic vertebra, 1.5 cun lateral to the posterior midline.

Ganshu BL-18 (Transporting Point)

On the back, below the spinous process of the ninth thoracic vertebra, 1.5 cun lateral to the posterior midline.

Pishu BL-20 (Transporting Point)

On the back, below the spinous process of the eleventh thoracic vertebra, 1.5 cun lateral to the posterior midline.

Shenshu BL-23 (Transporting Point)

On the back, below the spinous process of the second lumbar vertebra, 1.5 cun lateral to the posterior midline.

Yongquan KI-1 (Well Point)

On the sole of the foot, in the depression appearing on the anterior part of the sole when the foot is in plantar flexion, between the second and third metatarsal bones, one-third of the distance from the webs of the toes to the heel.

Taixi KI-3 (Source Point)

On the medial side of the foot, at the midpoint between the prominence of the medial malleolus and Achilles Tendon.

Jianshi PC-5

On the anterior forearm, 3 cun superior to the transverse crease of the wrist, between the tendons of palmaris longus and flexor carpi radialis muscles.

Neiguan PC-6 (Connecting Point)

On the anterior forearm, 2 cun superior to the transverse crease of the wrist, between the tendons of palmaris longus and flexor carpi radialis muscles.

Daling PC-7 (Source Point)

In the depression in the middle of the transverse crease of the wrist, between the tendons of the palmaris longus and flexor carpi radialis muscles.

Laogong PC-8 (Spring Point)

On the palm, between the second and third metacarpal bones, where the tip of the middle finger touches when a fist is made.

Zhongchong PC-9 (Well Point)

At the centre of the tip of the middle finger.

Guanchong SJ-1 (Well Point)

On the lateral side of the ring finger, 0.1 cun posterior from the corner of the fingernail.

Zhigou SJ-6

On the dorsal side of the forearm, 3 cun proximal to the dorsal crease of the wrist, between the radius and ulnar.

Fengchi GB-20

In the posterior aspect of the neck, below the occipital bone, in the depression between the upper portion of sternocleidomastoid and the trapezius muscles.

Riyue GB-24 (Collecting Point of the Gallbladder)

On the anterior chest midclavicular line, in the seventh intercostal space, 4 cun lateral to the anterior midline

Jingmen GB-25 (Collecting Point of the Kidney)

On the lateral abdomen, at the lower border of the free end of the twelfth rib.

Yanglingquan GB-34 (Sea Point)

On the lateral side of the leg, in the depression anterior and inferior to the head of the fibula.

Zuqiaoyin GB-44 (Well Point)

On the lateral side of the fourth toe, 0.1 cun from the corner of the toenail.

Dadun LR-1 (Well Point)

On the lateral side of the big toe, 0.1 cun from the corner of the toenail.

Xingjian LR-2 (Spring Point)

On the instep of the foot, between the first and second toes, at the junction of the red and white skin proximal to the margin of the web.

Taichong LR-3 (Source Point)

On the instep of the foot, in the depression distal to the junction of the first and second metatarsal bones.

Zhangmen LR-13 (Collecting Point of the Spleen)

On the lateral side of the abdomen, below the free end of the eleventh rib.

Qimen LR-14 (Collecting Point of the Liver)

On the chest, on the midclavicular line, in the sixth intercostal space, 4 cun lateral to the anterior midline.

Zhongwan RN-12 (Collecting Point of the Stomach)

The upper abdomen on the anterior midline, 4 cun above the centre of the umbilicus.

Jiuwei RN-15 (Connecting Point)

In the upper abdomen on the anterior midline, 1 cun inferior to the xyphoid process.

Mingmen DU-4

On the lumbar area, along the posterior midline, in the depression below the spinous process of the second lumbar vertebra.

Dazhui DU-14

On the back, along the posterior midline, in the depression below the spinous process of the seventh cervical vertebra.

Baihui DU-20

7 cun above the posterior hairline, on the midpoint of the line connecting the apexes of both ears.

Appendix C:
Chinese Names

导引养生功 Dǎoyǐn Yǎngshēng Gōng

Daoyin exercises for nourishing the Vital Principle
危机消除功 Wēijī Xiāochú Gōng
Stress Relief exercises

1.	太极调息	Tàijí Tiáoxī	Taiji Breathing
2.	顺水旋涡	Shùnshuǐ Xuánwō	Swirling Water
3.	鹰翥长空	Yīngzhù Chángkōng	Eagle Soaring in the Sky
4.	青龙献爪	Qīnglóng Xiànzhǎo	Black Dragon Displays Talons
5.	碧海藏龙	Bìhǎi Cánglóng	Dragon Hiding in the Blue Sea
6.	行云旋涡	Xíngyún Xuánwō	Swirling Clouds
7.	游鱼摆尾	Yóuyú Bǎiwěi	Swimming Fish Flaps Its Tail
8.	气沉丹田	Qìchén Dāntián	Sink Qi to Dantian

危机预防功 *Wēijī Yùfáng Gōng*
Stress Prevention exercises

1.	太极调息	Tàijí Tiáoxī	Taiji Breathing
2.	团扇遮月	Tuánshàn Zhēyuè	Round Fan Covers the Moon
3.	犁牛耕地	Líniú Gēngdì	Buffalo Ploughs the Land
4.	昭君梳发	Zhāojūn Shūfā	Distinguished Lord Combs Hair
5.	开花现佛	Kāihuā Xiànfó	Flower Displays Buddha
6.	单手托天	Dānshǒu Tuōtiān	One Hand Supports Heaven
7.	捶叩任督	Chuíkòu Rèndū	Tapping Rendu
8.	气沉丹田	Qìchén Dāntián	Sink Qi to Dantian

Daoyin Poem

夜 阑 人 静 万 虑 抛，

意 守 丹 田 封 七 窍。

呼 吸 徐 缓 搭 鹊 桥，

身 轻 如 燕 飘 云 霄。

Yèlán rénjìng wàn lǜ pāo,

Yì shǒu Dāntián fēng qīqiào.

Hūxī xúhuǎn dā Quèqiáo,

Shēn qīng rú yàn piāo yúnxiāo.

In the late evening stillness leave all troubles behind,

Set the mind on Dantian and seal the seven openings.

Breathe gently and unhurried and raise the magpie bridge,

With the body light as a swallow soaring through the skies.

Glossary

Acupoint   Acupoints are points situated along the energy channels of the body that can be used in acupuncture, acupressure and Qigong to control the flow of Qi.

Acupressure   The application of pressure to acupoints in order to affect the Qi flow.

Acupuncture   The use of needles on acupoints to control the flow of Qi.

Anqiao   Anqiao is a form of self-administered acupressure which results from the raising and lowering of the fingers and toes by flexing the wrists and ankles and this, in turn, exerts an influence through the source points on the internal organs.

Blood   In Traditional Chinese Medicine Blood (Xue) is not the same as what the West calls blood. Although Blood is sometimes identifiable with the blood of Western medicine, its characteristics and functions are not the same. Blood and Qi are inseparable. Blood is the "mother" of Qi; it carries Qi and also provides nutrients for its movement. In turn, Qi is the "commander" of the blood in that it is the force that makes blood flow throughout the body. Blood and Qi are the Yin and Yang of each other.

Breathing   In Qigong, which can be translated as breathing exercise, there are many different types of breathing patterns. However, abdominal breathing is the main type and there are two kinds which are Normal and Reverse Breathing, sometimes called Buddhist Breathing and Daoist Breathing respectively. Abdominal breathing refers to respiration which involves the expansion and contraction of the abdomen. In normal abdominal breathing the abdomen expands on the inhale and contracts on the exhale, which is said to be an efficient method of gathering energy, while reverse abdominal breathing has the abdomen contracting on the inhale and expanding on the exhale which is considered to be an efficient method of moving energy.

Channels   See *Jingluo*.

Collecting Points   Acupoints on the chest and abdomen where the Qi of the respective zangfu organs is infused.

Connecting Points   Each of the 12 primary channels has a Connecting Channel which diverges from the primary channel at the Connecting Point. In addition there are three further connecting points: one for the Conception vessel, one for the Governing vessel and one which is the great connecting point of the Spleen.

Cun   In acupuncture this is an anatomical "inch" which is proportional to a person's body. It is the measure of the width of a person's thumb at the knuckle.

Dantian   There are three main energy centres in the body. The Lower Dantian, in the lower abdomen, stores essence, the Middle Dantian, in the chest, stores energy and the Upper Dantian, in the head, stores spirit.

Dao   The Dao (also Tao), the path or way, is the name given to the universe, all that is seen and unseen, before the beginning and after the end; everything is Dao. Every possibility and every process is Dao. It is the goal of every enlightened person to be in harmony with the Dao, now and forever.

Daoyin   Therapeutic gymnastics. A system of healthcare based on physical exercise that is the oldest recorded category of Qigong.

External pathogens   Traditional Chinese Medicine categorizes six types of external pathogens. These are Wind, Heat, Cold, Damp, Dryness and Summer Heat, and are named after weather phenomena which possess similar characteristics.

Fire   In Traditional Chinese Medicine Fire is an extreme case of pathogenic Heat.

Five Elements   The Five Elements (Wuxing), or Five Phases, is a system used to describe the dynamic interactions and relationships between phenomena.

G.A.S.   The General Adaptive Syndrome (G.A.S.), more commonly known as the stress syndrome, is the mechanism by which the body confronts stress.

Holism   In medicine holism refers to the idea that mind and body, psyche and soma, cannot be separated from one another and that the holistic approach to health requires both aspects to be taken fully into account.

Jingluo   The channels or energy web of the body. It connects the upper, lower, exterior and interior parts of the body together. This web also connects all the internal organs and is the pathway for Qi and Blood.

Longevity   See *Yangsheng*.

Magpie bridge   The Daoyin Poem instructs to "raise the magpie bridge." Raising the magpie bridge (da queqiao) refers to a Chinese legend about a host of magpies that created a living bridge across the heavens so that a young cow-herder and his love, the weaving maiden, could meet. In Daoyin it refers to placing the tongue on the roof of the mouth in order to connect (bridge) the Yin and Yang channels.

Mechanism (of action)   Here the "mechanism of action" denotes the processes by which Daoyin exercises achieve their stated function.

Meridian   See *Jingluo*.

Original Qi   Original Qi (Yuan-Qi) or Congenital Qi is the energy we are born with. It is the inherited essence from our parents and is finite in quantity.

Phlegm   In Traditional Chinese Medicine Damp is one of the external pathogenic factors and this can congeal into Phlegm. There are two types of Phlegm: *substantial* Phlegm which is similar to the Western concept of phlegm i.e. sputum, and *insubstantial* Phlegm which is thought to be a thin pathological fluid which tends to accumulate in the channels and causes blockages.

Qi   Qi can be translated as energy, breath or steam but is mainly considered to be the energy that drives the universe and exists in everything.

Qi Stagnation   In Traditional Chinese Medicine if there is a blockage in the energy system it causes Qi Stagnation and when this Stagnation occurs it can lead to a multitude of health problems. In chronic stress it is Liver-Qi Stagnation that normally occurs.

Qigong   An umbrella term for thousands of different types of breathing and/or energy exercises current in China.

Sea Points   Acupoints where the Qi of the channel is most flourishing.

Seven openings   The Daoyin Poem instructs to "seal the seven openings." The seven openings (qiqiao) are the ears, eyes, nostrils and mouth, and refer to the senses which need to be turned inwards in order to consolidate our energy and develop an inner awareness by listening, smelling, looking and tasting inwards.

Source Points   In acupuncture each of the Twelve Regular Channels has a Source Point in the extremities where the Original Qi surfaces and lingers.

Spring Points   Acupoints where the Qi of the channel starts to flourish.

Stress   Stress is the body's reaction to being under pressure. This can be useful, for example to motivate someone to perform better, but if the pressure is prolonged it can lead to chronic stress which damages the mind and body.

Stressor   The cause of stress.

Taiji   The Chinese philosophy of Taiji, great extremes, is concerned with the dynamic interplay between two opposite but complementary forces known as Yin and Yang.

Taijiquan Taijiquan is a system of Wushu and healthcare based on the philosophy of Taiji.

Three Regulations The requirement that differentiates Qigong from other types of exercise is known as the "Three Regulations" (san tiao). This refers to the three methods employed simultaneously to improve an individual's health, i.e. the regulation of the body, the regulation of the breath and the regulation of the mind.

Transporting Points Acupoints on the back of the body where the Qi of the respective organs is infused and these points, therefore, affect their related organs directly. These points are particularly important for the treatment of chronic illnesses.

Well Points Acupoints located at the tips of the fingers and toes (except for Yongquan KI-1) where the channels are closest to the body surface. Energy at these points can be dynamic and unstable due to its change of state from Yang to Yin and vice versa. Therefore, these can be used in Daoyin to influence Qi flows throughout the body and organs. These points also have a strong effect on mental and emotional states and are often unconsciously used by finger tapping and using things like worry beads or Chinese health balls.

Wushu Chinese boxing. Literally, "martial arts" in Chinese.

Wuxing See *Five Elements*.

Yang See *Taiji*.

Yangqiao mai One of the extraordinary energy channels which functions alongside the Yinqiao mai to balance Yin and Yang in the body.

Yangsheng Yangsheng is the name given to the system of physical cultivation and longevity techniques for nourishing life. The methods of self-cultivation include Daoyin (therapeutic gymnastics), breath cultivation, dietetics, sexual cultivation and meditation.

Yin See *Taiji*.

Yinqiao mai One of the extraordinary energy channels which functions alongside the Yangqiao mai to balance Yin and Yang in the body.

Yuan-Qi See *Original Qi*.

Zangfu The collective term for the internal organs. The zang organs are the Kidneys, Liver, Heart, Spleen and Lungs and are categorized as Yin. The fu organs are the Bladder, Gallbladder, Small Intestine, Stomach and Large Intestine and are categorized as Yang.

Index

Anqiao movements 185–6
anus
  raising the 189–90

Baihui DU-20 acupoint 38,
  39, 40, 89, 91, 92, 234
ball holding position 30, 71,
  72, 73
basic movement
  hand positions 27–30
Black Dragon Displays Talons
  exercise
  acupoints utilized 201
  Daoyin bodywork 202
  Daoyin mind 203
  purpose of 201
  Seated Stress Relief 102–8
  Side Stepping 202
  Standing Stress Relief
    53–62
body
  regulation of 187
breathing
  and energy pulsation
    189–90
  regulation of 187–8
Buffalo Ploughs the Land
  exercise
  acupoints utilized 212
  Daoyin bodywork 212
  Daoyin mind 213
  Diagonal Stepping 212
  purpose of 211
  Seated Stress Prevention
    159–65
  Standing Stress Prevention
    133–7

cancer
  and Qigong 9–10
Chengzhen, Sima 24
closed palm position 27
Cross-over Stepping 34, 191
  and Round Fan Covers the
    Moon exercise 210

Dabao SP-21 acupoint 213,
  217, 219, 231
Dadun LR-1 acupoint 190,
  210, 213, 215, 216,
  233
Daling PC-7 acupoint 197,
  198, 199, 200, 203,
  204, 207, 212, 214,
  217, 218, 232
Daoyin Stepping
  characteristics of 35
  Cross-over Stepping 34,
    191
  Diagonal Stepping 30–1,
    190–1
  Side Stepping 32–3, 190
Daoyin tu (Daoyin Exercises
  Illustrated) 24
Daoyin Yangsheng
  background to 23–6
  and Traditional Chinese
    Medicine 25–6
  and Qi flow 23
  as form of Qigong 15, 186
  and Yang and Yin 191
Daozang 23
Dazhui DU-14 acupoint 198,
  218, 219, 220, 234

Diagonal Stepping 30–1,
  190–1
  and Buffalo Ploughs the
    Land exercise 212
  and Eagle Soaring in the
    Sky exercise 200
  and Flower Displays
    Buddha exercise 216
  and Swimming Fish Flaps
    Its Tail exercise 207
  and Swirling Water
    exercise 197
Distinguished Lords Combs
  Hair exercise
  acupoints utilized 213
  Daoyin bodywork 214
  Daoyin mind 215
  purpose of 213
  Seated Stress Prevention
    165–70
  Side Stepping 214
  Standing Stress Prevention
    137–42
Dragon Hiding in the Blue
  Sea exercise
  acupoints utilized 203
  Daoyin bodywork 204
  Daoyin mind 204
  purpose of 203
  Seated Stress Relief
    109–12
  Side Stepping 204
  Standing Stress Relief
    62–7

Eagle Soaring in the Sky
    exercise
  acupoints utilized
    199–200
  Daoyin bodywork 200–1
  Daoyin mind 201
  Diagonal Stepping 200
  purpose of 199
  Seated Stress Relief
    97–102
  Standing Stress Relief
    46–53
Earth controls Water 150,
    180, 217
energy system
  channel system for 228
  and Dantians 228–9
  and the Five Element
    theory 227–8

Feishu BL-13 acupoint 213,
    231
Fengchi GB-20 acupoint
    199–200, 201, 203,
    233
Fenglong ST-40 acupoint
    199, 200, 203, 230
Fire controls Metal 137, 164,
    211, 212
Fire from the Heart 67, 102,
    112
Fire from the Liver 62, 67,
    74, 102, 108, 112, 116
Five Element theory 221–5,
    227–8
Flower Displays Buddha
    exercise
  acupoints utilized 215
  Daoyin bodywork 216
  Daoyin mind 217
  purpose of 215
  Seated Stress Prevention
    170–5
  Standing Stress Prevention
    142–6

Ganshu BL-18 acupoint 199,
    200, 201, 202, 231
Guanchong SJ-1 acupoint
    201, 210, 215, 233
Guangde, Zhang 25

hand positions 27–30
Hegu LI-4 acupoint 80, 121,
    146, 175, 207, 213,
    214, 230
hollow fist position 29
Huang Di Nei Jing Ling Shu
    (The Yellow Emperor's
    Internal Classic: Spiritual
    Pivot) 185

Jianshi PC-5 acupoint 199,
    200, 203, 232
Jiexi ST-41 acupoint 197,
    207, 230
Jimen SP-11 acupoint 57, 59,
    62, 105, 107, 108
Jin, Zhou 13–14
Jingmen GB-25 acupoint
    215, 216, 233
Jiuwei RN-15 acupoint 80,
    121, 151, 152, 153,
    181, 182, 183, 207,
    219, 220, 234

Kang, Xi 24

Laogong PC-8 acupoint 40,
    46, 67, 80, 92, 97,
    121, 137, 143, 165,
    171, 192, 197, 198,
    199, 203, 207, 208,
    212, 215, 216, 232
Liver-Qi Stagnation 62, 74,
    108, 116, 195, 201
Lower Dantian 39, 83, 85,
    86, 87, 90, 91, 124,
    125, 126, 127, 150,
    179, 192, 193, 194,
    195, 198, 199, 206,
    220, 229

Maggie's Cancer Caring
    Centres 9, 13
magpie bridge 189
Metal controls Wood 170,
    213
Middle Dantian 83, 84, 85,
    86, 124, 125, 126,
    127, 194, 228–9
mind
  regulation of 188–9

Mingmen DU-4 acupoint 53,
    102, 133, 151, 152,
    153, 159, 181, 182,
    183, 200, 201, 210,
    211, 219, 220, 234

Neiguan PC-6 acupoint 70,
    72, 73, 74, 113–14,
    115, 116, 205, 206,
    232

One Hand Supports Heaven
    exercise
  acupoints utilized 217
  Daoyin bodywork 218
  Daoyin mind 218–19
  purpose of 217
  Seated Stress Prevention
    176–9
  Side Stepping 218
  Standing Stress Prevention
    147–50
open palm position 29

pelvis
  tilting the 189–90
Phlegm 67, 112, 200
physical fitness
  Western concept of 15–16
Pishu BL-20 acupoint 199,
    200, 231

Qigong
  and cancer sufferers 9–10
  and Daoyin Yangsheng
    15, 186
  in Chinese hospitals
    11–12
  and energy pulsation
    189–90
  forms of 15
  Three Regulations 187–9
Qigong Principles of Action
  Anqiao movements 185–6
  and Taiji Breathing 192–3
Qimen LR-14 acupoint 143,
    171, 201, 202, 205,
    215, 216, 234

Riyue GB-24 acupoint 215,
216, 233
Round Fan Covers the Moon
exercise
acupoints utilized 210
Daoyin bodywork 210–11
Daoyin mind 211
purpose of 209–10
Seated Stress Prevention
154–9
Standing Stress Prevention
128–33

Seated Stress Prevention
exercises
Buffalo Ploughs the Land
159–65
Distinguished Lord Combs
Hair 165–70
Flower Displays Buddha
170–5
One Hand Supports
Heaven 176–9
Round Hand Covers the
Moon 154–9
Sink Qi to Dantian 183
Taiji Breathing 154
Tapping Rendu 180–3
Seated Stress Relief exercises
Black Dragon Displays
Talons 102–8
Dragon Hiding in the Blue
Sea 109–12
Eagle Soaring in the Sky
97–102
Sink Qi to Dantian 121–7
Swimming Fish Flaps Its
Tail 116–21
Swirling Clouds 112–16
Swirling Water 93–7
Taiji Breathing 88–93
shang fist position 29
Shangyang LI-1 acupoint 29,
142, 170, 201, 210,
213, 215, 216, 230
Shaochong HT-9 acupoint
199, 201, 203, 204,
210, 212, 231
Shaofu HT-8 acupoint 199,
203, 204, 212, 231
Shaoshang LU-11 acupoint
29, 201, 210, 213,
215, 216, 230

Shaoze SI-1 acupoint 201,
210, 215, 231
Shenmen HT-7 acupoint 197,
198, 207, 212, 213,
214, 217, 218, 231
Shenshu BL-23 acupoint
210, 211, 232
Side Stepping 32–3, 190
and Black Dragon Displays
Talons exercise 202
and Distinguished Lord
Combs Hair exercise
214
and Dragon Hiding in the
Blue Sea exercise 204
and One Hand Supports
Heaven exercise 218
and Round Fan Covers the
Moon exercise 210
and Swirling Clouds
exercise 205
and Tapping Rendu
exercise 219
Sink Qi to Dantian exercises
and Qigong Principles of
Action 193–5
Seated Stress Prevention
183
Seated Stress Relief 121–7
Standing Stress Prevention
153
Standing Stress Relief
80–7
Standing Stress Prevention
exercises
Buffalo Ploughs the Land
133–7
Distinguished Lord Combs
Hair 137–42
Flower Displays Buddha
142–6
One Hand Supports
Heaven 147–50
Round Fan Covers the
Moon 128–33
Sink Qi to Dantian 153
Tapping Rendu 150–3
Taiji Breathing 128
Standing Stress Relief
exercises
Black Dragon Displays
Talons 53–62
Dragon Hiding in the Blue
Sea 62–7

Eagle Soaring in the Sky
46–53
Sink Qi to Dantian 80–7
Swimming Fish Flaps Its
Tail 74–80
Swirling Clouds 67–74
Swirling Water 41–6
Taiji Breathing 36–41
stress
in Traditional Chinese
Medicine 195–6
definition of 18–19
and five-stage stress model
21–2
as non-specific illness
17–18
and three-stage stress
model 19–21
Stress Prevention exercises
Standing Stress Prevention
exercises 128–53
and Yin 21–2
Stress Relief exercises
Seated Stress Relief
exercises 88–127
Standing Stress Relief
exercises 36–87
and Yang 21–2
Swimming Fish Flaps Its Tail
exercise
acupoints utilized 207
Daoyin bodywork 207
Daoyin mind 208
Diagonal Stepping 207
purpose of 206
Seated Stress Relief
116–21
Standing Stress Relief
74–80
Swirling Clouds exercise
acupoints utilized 205
Daoyin bodywork 206
Daoyin mind 206
purpose of 205
Seated Stress Relief
112–16
Side Stepping 205
Standing Stress Relief
67–74
Swirling Water exercise
acupoints utilized 197
Daoyin bodywork 198
Daoyin mind 199
Diagonal Stepping 197

Swirling Water exercise *cont.*
  purpose of 197
  Seated Stress Relief 93–7
  Standing Stress Prevention
    128
  Standing Stress Relief
    41–6

Taibai SP-3 acupoint 190,
  213, 214, 217, 218,
  230
Taichong LR-3 acupoint 190,
  197, 199, 200, 201,
  203, 205, 207, 213,
  214, 215, 216, 234
Taiji Breathing exercises
  and Qigong Principles of
    Action 192–3
  Seated Stress Prevention
    154
  Seated Stress Relief 88–93
  Standing Stress Prevention
    128
  Standing Stress Relief
    36–41
Taiqing daoyin yangsheng jing
  (*Great Clarity Scripture
  of Daoyin and Nourishing
  Life*) 24
Taixi KI-3 acupoint 191, 197,
  207, 210, 212, 213,
  215, 216, 217, 218, 232
Taiyuan LU-9 acupoint 213,
  217, 219, 230
Tapping Rendu exercises
  acupoints utilized 219
  Daoyin bodywork 219–20
  Daoyin mind 220
  purpose of 219
  Seated Stress Prevention
    180–3
  Side Stepping 219
  Standing Stress Prevention
    150–3
Three Regulations 187–9,
  192

Upper Dantian 86, 126, 228

Wood controls Earth 146,
  175, 215
Water controls Fire 133, 159,
  204, 210

World Health Organization
  (WHO) 16

Xiaozhoutian 189
Xingjian LR-2 acupoint 57,
  59, 62, 105, 107, 108,
  199, 200, 201, 202,
  203, 205, 233
Xinshu BL-15 acupoint 198,
  231
Xiuzhen jingyi zalun
  (*Miscellaneous Discourses
  on the Essential Meaning
  of Cultivating Perfection*)
  24

Yang
  and breathing 188
  and Daoyin exercises 191
  as physical response to
    stress 19, 20
  and Stress Relief exercises
    21–2, 36
Yanglingquan GB-34
  acupoint 199, 200,
  201, 203, 205
Yangsheng lun (*On Nourishing
  Life*) 24
Yen, Zou 221
Yin
  and breathing 188
  and Daoyin exercises 191
  as mental response to stress
    19, 20
  and Stress Prevention
    exercises 21–2, 128
Yinbai SP-1 acupoint 190,
  197, 207, 210, 213,
  214, 217, 218, 230
Yongquan KI-1 acupoint 191,
  192, 193, 194, 197,
  207, 210, 212, 215,
  216, 232

Zhangmen LR-13 acupoint
  201, 202, 205, 215,
  216, 217, 219, 234
Zhigou SJ-6 acupoint 70,
  72, 73, 113, 115, 205,
  206, 233
Zhongchong PC-9 acupoint
  210, 215, 232

Zhongwan RN-12 acupoint
  199, 200, 234
Zhubing yuanhou lun (*Treatise
  on the Causes and
  Symptoms of Diseases*) 24
Zuqiaoyin GB-44 acupoint
  74, 116, 205, 233